Get Rich Quick, Build Wealth Now
Copyright © 2018 by Mbok Antoine

All rights reserved. No part of this book may be reproduced or transmitted in any form or by any means without written permission from the author.

ISBN (9781795293686)

Rich Quick Build Wealth Now

Testimonials

What others are saying about this book:

I now feel I too can be rich.
Nandu Mulder

I wish I read this book years ago, it's so practical. **C. Jansen**

I love it I love it I love, so inspiring. **J. Thomas**

Get Rich Quick Build Wealth Now

TRUST THAT BEING RICH IS BETTER.

MOTIVATIONAL BOOK

Author: Antoine Mbok

FIRST EDITION

SEPTEMBER 23RD 2018

INDEPENDENTLY PUBLISHED

Antoine Mbok

PO Box 22506 Windhoek, Namibia 9000

Tel. GSM: +264 81 306 2741 E-mail: antoinembok@gmail.com

Get Rich Quick Build Wealth Now

MOTIVATIONAL BOOK

Author: Antoine Mbok

FIRST EDITION

SEPTEMBER 23RD 2018

INDEPENDENTLY PUBLISHED

Antoine Mbok

PO Box 22506 Windhoek, Namibia 9000

Tel. GSM: +264 81 306 2741 E-mail: antoinembok@gmail.com

All rights reserved. No part of this book may be reproduced or transmitted in any form or by any means, electronic or mechanical, including photocopying, recording or by any information storage and retrieval system, without written permission from the author, except for the inclusion of brief quotations in a review.

Copyright © 2018 by Antoine Mbok:
First Edition, 2018

DEDICATION

This book is dedicated to all my children; Tamia, Toni, Antoine III, Richard Reinhart, Pierre Andrew, Genesis Devine, Junior Carl Mathys, Ousies Mathys, Jules Walter, Valentina, Sylvain Anthony Geraldt, Sean Henry, Stacey Suzanne, Marie-France, Francisco Martins, Nefertari Nadia, Paul Joseph and Laurentine Agnes Marthe, babies you are truly the catalyst in my life. Through snow, hail, desert scotching sun, storms, I keep going, I soldier on, I take the blow, despite multiple failures, persecutions and prosecutions I have had to endure, I am still here because of you. Time and again I have been knocked down and had to look up, stand up, dust up and keep going not knowing where the energy was coming from. After many restarts I came to realize that you, my children give me hope, the will to live and that energy when I am down or just when I need it to bounce back stronger and more determined.

This book is a critical tool for today's society, a sort of survival guide in this capitalistic jungle of numbers, interest rates, inflation, profits and loses, return on investment and so on. We learn at school, through experience and through others by inspiration. I would want you to have the best tools you need to succeed in life, having the right mind set as recommended in this book. You are the reason I set out to write this book, the motivation to push for my dream of writing this book to become a reality. I pray and thank GOD for every nano second for my life while placing a lot of hopes on my children.

I am absolutely certain that all my dreams and aspirations through all of you will come true. Whatever I could not accomplish you will, whatever I could not become you will be.

I unconditionally love you.

Daddy.

EPIGRAPH

I live by these words as they help me define success in the most just manner, and equally help me keep happiness within reach.

Success is to be measure not so much by the position that one has reached in life as by the obstacles which he has overcome while trying to succeed.

By: Booker T. Washington

Get Rich Quick Build Wealth Now

Table of Contents

About the author	Page 9-10
Preface	Page 12-15
Acknowledgements	Page 16-16
Chapter I Get Rich Quick	Page 17-38
Chapter II Build Wealth Now	Page 39-51
Chapter III The Pursuit of Happiness	Page 52-56
Chapter IV Dream Killers	Page 57-63
Chapter V How Money Works	Page 64-74
Chapter VI Psychological Conditioning	Page 75-81
Chapter VII Principles of Building Wealth	Page 82-84
Chapter VIII Success & Inspirations	Page 85-95
Appendix	Page 96-98
Ressources	Page 99-101
Bibliography	Page 102-104
Index & Glossary	Page 105-106

About The Author

His Majesty Mbok Antoine, Chief of the Bassa Community in Mbankomo, Cameroon, CEO of MINVESTCO. Born in Douala, Cameroon on August 2nd 1973, Son of former Cameroonian Police Inspector Antoine Mbok and of Pharmacy Technician Assistant Amandjou Suzanne, Grandson of New Bell Bassa, Douala Traditional Chief Mbog Nonga Pierre.  I received elementary and primary education in Cameroon, Secondary education in France and the United States and finally university studies with Columbia Union College in Takoma Park Maryland, U.S.A. Initially registered as a Pre-medical student studying to be a radiologist, I changed my major at a later stage to business administration as well as Investment banking. As a student I won awards, made the honor roll and have been fortunate to benefit from a very high IQ. Worked in the US since the early age of 16 while still in High School and worked as a professional for various blue chip US companies. I am an entrepreneur and have been most of my life; creating, managing and investing in various businesses, being in business made me rich. Being rich opened up doors and gave me the opportunities often not available to most people. I have failed many times in business and my family life divorcing twice, I have had to reinvent myself so many times due to life changing situations and that made me stronger every time. Life has not been easy for me at all and for anyone thinking my background, grandson of a Chief and studies abroad reveals a life with a silver spoon you are very much wrong I had a wooden spoon. I live in Namibia, a country where customer complaints have landed me in provisional police custody for months at a time, disrupting and destroying my businesses, credit worthiness, scattering my children, friends and family but I have had to look up, stand up, dust up again and again; walking around with tarnished pride and being an occasional victim of xenophobia attacks, discrimination and bias. I dream of a better life for everyone and I am interested in contributing to a better life for my fellow men, women and children. We can always do better and I would like to motivate everyone to bring out their best and build together a society that will observe African values, cultures and traditions.

I have been exposed to so much in my life and acquired experience that I would like to share with my children and the world.

Foreword

Preface

"Get Rich Quick, Build Wealth Now" that is the title I chose for this book. I had my doubts about the title; first of all it is long and secondly I thought many people will immediately turn away once they read Get Rich Quick believing this is a book about a get rich quick scheme and everyone knows, get rich quick schemes never really workout in the end. I decided nevertheless to keep the title because the words quick and now being part of the title were meant to express the urgency with which people need to act in their objective of getting rich and building wealth. The book's title is basically like an order, an imperative directive you are being given; a boot camp kind of language. There are a thousand and one books out there published with the aim of motivating people or teaching people how to build wealth or get rich. I bought many of those books and studied them with passion because my aim when I retire is to have billionaire status but there has always been something missing from the books I bought as if the authors never mean for me to really acquire the skills I truly need to build wealth. It seemed to me that these books just wanted to give you a taste to let you have an ah ha! Moment and hook you into buying a lot of other books, tapes, programs, plans and other supposed tools to build wealth.

I come from a modest family, we have had our ups and downs poverty has always been at our doorsteps knocking hard but we have always managed. The wealth building principles I have learned and acquired were not practiced in our family, it's our paternal grandfather's chief status that gave us the edge and nobility we have known. We did not receive financial education of any kind from our parents, so you can imagine that it's been hard, very hard to build wealth without the knowledge I have since acquired and I am sharing in this book. When my paternal grandfather passed away his children lost the edge, part of the nobility and did not or could not capitalize on the status of their father, leading many to become the average Joes, back in the lot of the population. As a grandson of a Chief and strong man I truly believe that I have inherited my grandfather's spirit, strength and perhaps luck because although I was very young I remember and live by words I heard him pronounce which unfortunately I will not share with the world but these words have made me what I am today. I have failed a thousand and one times but I never settle for less than I felt I should have and my drive took me to places I could gain knowledge about building wealth. I read books, went to seminars, studied rich people and took courses to qualify as a Financial Planner and stock broker. I never missed an episode of "the lifestyle of the rich and Famous" with Robin Leach and I often cried of joy or envy , I never really knew why I shed tears when I watched that show especially at the end when Dion Warwick's beautiful voice made me day dream about being rich. I come from a modest but noble family of chiefs; initially my grandfather until his death and then my father who unfortunately mismanaged his tenure and lost both the respect and nobility that came with the position because he could not manage it and in fact abandoned the family he was supposed to lead. The noble blue blood I have has me following in the footsteps of my grandfather and father as I am now a chief myself and I not only have responsibility to my family but I also have the responsibility to lead an entire community. Managing a community in Africa is not an easy thing as the chief is consulted for everything and has to intervene in people's lives but one of my first thoughts has been to see a community that is prosperous because a financially comfortable community will have less complaints, less corrupt and immoral behaviors. This book is dedicated to my community in general and my children in particular and I want them to have the values promoted in this book because they encompass the time honored principles of wealth building and management. These were my really strong motivations for writing this book and insuring that I would be transmitting quality information for my people and family.

I practice what I preach, I feel rich and I am building wealth. I am destined to achieve greatness and I will by God's grace and by my works I will reach the destiny I see for myself; I will be a billionaire.

I have been self-employed, an entrepreneur and business owner for the most part of my life, I only worked for large American multinationals when I was much younger but since the age of 26, I have been master of my time and driver of my destiny. Being self-employed is best when trying to build great wealth but not the only thing because you can be employed and become rich through your employer. I walked a different path, choose yours and this book makes a lot of suggestions to help you make the right decisions.

With so many books claiming to teach people how to build wealth, get rich or how to invest being published for years, many people often ask; why don't we have a lot of rich people? Statistics still show a large majority of people living above their means and people living paycheck to paycheck. I have concluded that many of those books are simply sales brochures, hooks, baits to bring people into a program that will keep them spending more and more money, supposedly to improve themselves or acquire the skills needed to become rich. Many of these authors' books will want you to get into some kind of a plan and sale you various additional products; if not audio tapes, CDs, seminars, webinars, podcast memberships, an investment plan or the next edition of their book. To the authors of these books you will never be ready enough to actually start building wealth and sometimes they will create deliberate complications or formulas in their books forcing you to look for the next clue in their next edition to understand. You are not a fool, just pick up any book out there claiming to teach you how to build wealth and see what hides behind the book so that is what makes the difference with this book, Get Rich Quick, Build Wealth Now, we give you the best advice out there, time honored, tried and tested methods of building wealth and we place in your hands. If this books does not make you rich quick, then nothing will. The information contained in this book is worth billions or trillions if you have aspirations to build wealth like the Rothschild family. In this book we get you to set your mind right for building riches, we take away or at least point to the usual hurdles keeping people from building great wealth, we give you the fundamentals of building riches and we provide you with suggestions on how to manage, save and invest your money. This book prepares you to the wealthy lifestyle and the right attitude to have towards money. Yes, yes, yes, believe that money changes people just as power corrupts people, money absolutely changes people and the changes can be devastating if you don't manage being wealthy properly. There are real life stories of multi-millionaires who lost all and ended up living with poverty at their door steps because they did not master being wealthy. This book will give you your master's degree in getting rich and building wealth if you absorb all information provided.

This book has no catch and reveals everything you need to know to Get rich Quick and Build Wealth Now. Join me to the top, will you? See you at the top.

Mbok Antoine
Author

Acknowledgements

I would like to thank all who encouraged me and motivated me to work hard and come up with this concept and book that will change the lives of many people for the best. As referenced, many websites and authors of various works have been quoted for illustration and for inspiration like; Robert Kiyosaki, Katherine Hurst, Brian Tracy, Grant Cardone, www.forbes.com, Wikipedia, Google, Investopedia, www.cnbc.com, www.blackenterprises.com, www.psychologytoday.com to name a few that have allowed me to save money and time in doing research to confirm facts for this book. To list everyone that inspired this book would require more space than is available. I am grateful to family (my mother, Amandjou Suzanne, Sister, Anastasie Mbono and all my children), friends, co-workers, my enemies (or haters), many websites, various departments of various governments from England to South Africa, Cameroon, Namibia, USA and France, libraries, industrial institutions, periodicals and many individuals whose names I don't even know. All information contained in this book from various sources fall in the Public domain category in terms of copyright, published or unpublished works from other authors quoted herein for illustration is used as permitted under the US Fair Use section of the Copyright Law and the Berne Convention, Article 10 (copyright exceptions).

Warning—Disclaimer

This book is a motivational tool designed to provide information on how to get rich and build wealth through prudent fiscal management and having a positive wealth building mentality. It is sold with the understanding that the publisher and author are not engaged in rendering personal finance management, legal, accounting or other professional services. It is not the purpose of this book to reprint all the information that is otherwise available to authors and/or publishers in the public domain, but instead to complement, amplify and supplement other texts. Some information in this book from other authors fall in the public domain, published or unpublished works from other authors quoted for illustration are used as permitted under the US Fair Use section of the Copyright Law and the Berne Convention for the Protection of Literacy and Artistic Works of 1886, specifically Article 10 (copyright exceptions).

You are urged to read all the available material, learn as much as possible about financial management and wealth building, and tailor the information to your individual needs. This book is not a get-rich-quick scheme and only provides readers with the author's personal experience, opinion and concept in getting rich and building wealth through a positive mental attitude about money and wealth.

Every effort has been made to make this book as complete and as accurate as possible. However, there may be mistakes, both typographical and in content. Therefore, this book should be used only as a general guide. Furthermore, this book contains information on fiscal management, personal finance management, neuro linguistic programming and wealth building mentality that is current only up to the printing date.

The purpose of this book is to motivate, educate and entertain. The author, printer, publisher and distributor shall have neither liability nor responsibility to any person or entity with respect to any loss or damage caused, or alleged to have been caused, directly or indirectly, by the information contained in this book.

If you do not wish to be bound by the above, you may return this book through the Publisher only, for a full refund from publisher within 3 days from date of purchase.

Get Rich Quick Build Wealth Now

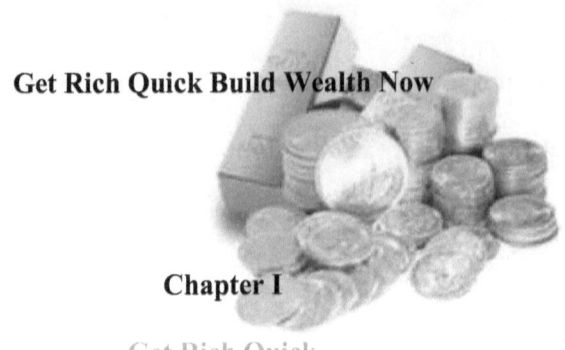

Chapter I

Get Rich Quick

Get rich quick, why wait? If you were born rich or have been rich and somehow your fortunes turned around in this traitorous capitalistic environment and you become poor or if you have known poverty and you succeeded in becoming rich, then you know: being rich is betterrrrrrrrrr!!! If you have been rich and you've been poor. Then you know both sides very well. When you are poor you know you want to be rich therefore no one should ever succeed in convincing you that somehow being poor is your ticket to heaven or just having enough is the right way to live because it's not. Besides fictional characters no rich person has ever wished to be poor. We have heard of rich people donating their fortunes to charity but no one that is rich has ever wished to be poor. If you have anyone like that around you preaching that being rich is a sin or having just enough is the way God meant it, get as far away from them as possible, they are wrong, god meant for you to live a healthy and prosperous life and he gave everyone the means to do so. Irrespective of your situation or condition, you can succeed and the simple truth to this is people like you in the same circumstance who made it rich, perhaps your class mates, your friends, a family member or even people with much less education than you. The more money you have the better life you will live and offer to your children, family, friends and community. Having money gives you true independence, the freedom to be whatever you can be and do whatever you want to do, when you want to do it. When your needs and wants are met you discover your true humanity and philanthropy. Money does change you completely, most of the time for the best but sometimes some people's worst comes out and this depends on how the wealth was acquired. Being rich is having money, enough money to satisfy all your wants and needs while being wealthy is not only having enough money and assets to satisfy all your wants and needs but also heaving a wealth mentality. Your definition of being rich or wealthy may differ from the above but accept this definition as strictly to put certain perspectives in this book into context. This chapter looks into getting rich, being rich and the motivations behind aspirations to riches, we also look at poverty and reveal the secret or should we say the difference between what makes the rich rich and what makes the poor poor.

To get rich or not to get, that is the question. But the answer to most people should be to be rich, and it is when polling a small group of people 9 out of 10 will clearly express their preference to being rich. Getting to being  rich seems to be the problem for most people who for the most part do not have a plan or strategy. The current political and economic system is not made to make millionaires out of everyone, imagine a situation where you work and get paid a large amount of money, say 3 million, would you want to keep working? Probably not. The system in place is made to keep people working getting paid just enough to cover expenses until the next paycheck. We live in modern day exploitative slavery, where the entire system is built to keep you in need paying you just enough to satisfy your needs and a few wants so you keep working and making the rich richer and paying government its taxes to keep it going as well. When we have numbers like 90% of the wealth being in the hands of 10% of the population that should have you understand that the rich will keep getting richer. The system, what we mean by the system is the political and economic environment is designed to keep you poor and spending so you keep needing more and more money. I am sure you have experienced a situation where when working and getting paid 3000 per month, that amount is just enough to feed you, shelter you and keep you going until the next paycheck but when you move on to a better position and now you are earning 10 times more say 30000 per month after sometime you find yourself in the same situation where that money allows you to feed yourself, by then you got a better more expensive shelter and have just enough to get you to your next paycheck. There are companies out there inventing products, that are practical for some but mostly extraneous for the majority and they spend a lot of money marketing products we don't really need to get our money away from us. Money is a great servant but a very very bad master, so we need to learn to master money and not be mastered by money. Being mastered by money is when despite making more money than before you find yourself still needing more and more money to satisfy your daily needs and wants.

The economic system being as it is makes it very difficult for people to break ranks and move from the exploitative slavery stage to the financially independent and rich stage. Having a full time job that allows you to satisfy your wants and needs does not often leave enough time for you to plan your escape out of the exploitative slavery stage. There are several books and wealth building systems that give you only half truths to keep you chasing after their books, tapes, podcasts and seminars so they make as much money as they can from you. Many books will simply be a bait to hook you and keep you wanting more and more information believing that you need continuous education to learn how to get rich. This book breaks ranks and provides you with time honored principles of wealth building. You will see that the principles in this book are self-evident and make sense and when implemented they work. The most important when setting out to do something is that you get results as you do it. But to build wealth you first need to learn how to get out of this modern day exploitative slavery that we are all in. whether you are poor or part of the middle class and even the upper class you are part of the modern day exploitative slavery, because to keep your social status you have to keep working, earning just enough to keep you in your social class and that does not make you different from anyone else trapped in the same system. Very often we see dramatic changes in people's lives when they lose their employment, you see them moving from a big house to a smaller house from a middle class neighborhood to a lower income neighborhood. If you work for a living, have a job or you are self-employed you are part of the modern day exploitative slavery, there is however great news in that, today getting rich and breaking away from the system to achieve financial independence is a matter of choices and behaviors, limitations exist but achieving riches whether you have education or are illiterate, handicapped or abled bodied you can make it.

Again being rich is having money, enough money to satisfy all your wants and needs while being wealthy is not only having money, enough money and assets to satisfy all your wants and needs but also heaving a wealth mentality. When you are wealthy if you work your money works harder than you do, you are on the other side of the system and exploit resources or people to keep your wealth growing. Your money does all the work. The definition above of being rich will assist us looking into how to Get rich quick, build wealth now. Notice that the book's title is GET rich quick not BE rich quick because we make the difference between being rich and getting rich, simply being rich means you are already there and getting rich in this book's context means you are still working on it, setting yourself up for riches. For anyone who thought this book is about a get rich quick scheme, oh well sorry to disappoint you it's much better than that. You will not only get rich and build wealth but it will be done in a sustained manner. In this book we are not yet rich we are getting to it and to get to being rich there are a number of things to learn, to do and a certain behavior to adopt.

Get rich quick is a suggestion that we should quickly be in a mental state of creating, growing and maintaining earnings so as to be rich, wealthy.

Here are our suggestions on how to Get Rich Quick, again in this book, it's how to quickly get into that mental state needed to create, build, maintain wealth so as to be rich, wealthy. To get Rich you must decide to be rich, even if you already have a million or two in your bank account, money has a funny way of changing your lifestyle, your wants and needs and unfortunately poverty is chasing everyone, every second of each day and has a way of catching up with you if you don't adopt a certain behavior and mentality. Poverty is real be it in the form of a spirit, aura or energy in fact it's in and around us; we call it in with the way we behave; poverty is a state of mind. There are many broke millionaires out there and many people who are known to have been very rich but today are part of the masses of poor people. What comes to mind is several stars, actors known to have earned millions, athletes who had multi-million deals and paydays but still ended up in the masses of the economically struggling class, back to the struggle, into the middle class or lower, back into the modern day exploitative slavery class. If 10 million fall into your laps today, you can consider yourself rich by any standard because you may never need to work again in your life but unfortunately that money may not last because it will change your lifestyle dramatically and poverty will be harder at work to bring you back. Sudden riches seldom last because people are caught off guard and did not prepare to receive that much money; they will want to satisfy all they wants and needs and will not measure the impact of the various changes in their lifestyle. New home in more affluent neighborhood needing more maintenance, picking up expensive habits from neighbors in affluent areas etc.....

The rich or wealth mentality you need to get rich, grow your wealth and stay rich is out there in the form of personal experience from various individuals who made it rich against all odds. There are hundreds of books focusing on helping people get into the mental state needed to be rich and stay rich, the best books are those that take into account the physiology of the brain, the energies or auras around us, for everything is made of energy and we cannot exclude the spirituality in anything we do or anything around us. There are books going as far as suggesting neuro-programming to get people to adopt positive thinking and the mentality to get rich and stay rich by listening to subliminal messages in audio recordings. Money, assets, poverty, being rich and wealthy are said to be energies, living energies that can be manipulated by our brain. Wanting something strong enough it seems puts you half way to getting your wish granted. Money has to be seduced attracted and made to feel it's wanted, needed and respected, like a relationship with a person. The best works out there have been summarized here for illustration only, we present the essence of works from accomplished authors and motivational speakers, it's important to understand that a shift in mentality and behavior are critical for anyone wanting to Get Rich.

The many wonderful works available and recommended include the book from Robert T. Kiyosaki, the author of Rich Dad, Poor Dad. Lessons from Rich Dad, Poor Dad are very telling as they demonstrate that many people work very hard, but they never seem to earn enough and they are trapped in what seems to be a sort of servitude, poverty is out to get everyone. Robert Kiyosaki explains how to escape the grip of perpetual poverty and capitalistic enslavement to achieve financial independence. Kiyosaki compares two fathers' attitudes, principles, ideas, financial practices, and approach in making and managing money. He compares his university educated poor dad to those people who are perpetually running in the what he calls The Rat Race, helplessly trapped by poverty in a vicious cycle of needing more but never able to satisfy their dreams for wealth because of the lack of financial literacy.

Kiyosaki presents six principal lessons that he learned:

- The rich don't work for money

Kiyosaki develops the ideas that the poor and the middle class work for money, fear and greed cause ignorance and poverty, and the importance of using one's emotions versus thinking with emotions.

- The importance of financial literacy

At a business meeting at the Edgewater Beach Hotel in Chicago, Charles Schwab, Samuel Insull, Howard Hopson, Ivar Kreuger, Leon Frazier, Richard Whitney, Arthur Cotton, Jesse Livermore and Albert Fall met to talk about different investments and money schemes. Twenty-five years later, a report stated that a large majority of those extremely wealthy people that met in Chicago either ended up in jail, dead or penniless. The major idea to take from the results of these unfortunate entrepreneurs is that you need financial literacy to be and stay safe. The idea that was represented with the big 1920's entrepreneurs is still prevalent today with some of the professional athletes making poor financial decisions and ending up with next to nothing. This specific lesson is meant to teach people not to be wise with your money once you have it, but rather be smart with your money before you have it. In a way, don't try to build a skyscraper or even a house without building a strong foundation first. According to Kiyosaki, there is one rule, and only rule that can help a person to build a strong foundation; know the difference between an asset and a liability, and make sure that you only control assets. He says, "Intelligence solves problems and produces money. Money without financial intelligence is money soon gone."

Kiyosaki believes that financial literacy begins with a working knowledge of accounting. It is essential to know the difference between assets and liabilities. To make these two terms understandable to readers, Kiyosaki makes a rudimentary diagram of these two concepts to motivate them to purchase assets in order to solidify the asset column, while keeping the liabilities (expenses) to a bare minimum. Kiyosaki states that poor people remain poor because they do the opposite. They pile up on their liabilities and have zero assets so that their balance sheets and income statements look out of kilter. People have to understand that it's not how much they make, but how much they keep according to the author.

- Minding Your own business

Kiyosaki remarks that individuals need to mind their own business if they wish to become financially self-sufficient. They shouldn't mind their employer's business, they should strive for ways to become their own boss and nurture their own businesses. To him, real assets are anything with value – stocks, bonds, mutual funds, income-producing real estate, notes, royalties from intellectual property, etc. This is accomplished by gaining knowledge of accounting, investing, understanding the markets, and the law. He says being ignorant gets you bullied whereas being informed translates into "you have a fighting chance."

- Taxes and corporations

The rich possess the knowledge and savoir faire to use the power of the corporation to protect and enhance their assets. The advantage of a corporation versus that of the individual lies in how corporations pay taxes, according to the author. Kiyosaki makes this point clearly: individuals earn money, pay taxes on that money, and live with what's left. The corporation, on the other hand, earns money, spends everything it can, and is taxed on anything that's left. Kiyosaki adds that the rich are hardly taxed.

- The rich invent money

He says that each person is born with talent but that talent is suppressed because of self-doubt and fear. He remarks that it's not necessarily the educated smart people who get ahead but the bold and adventurous. People never get ahead financially even if they have plenty of money because they have opportunities that they fail to tap, he stresses. Most of them just sit around waiting for opportunity to happen. The author's idea is that people create luck; they should not wait around for it. He says it's the same with money. It has to be created.

The author is clear by saying, "a trained mind is a rich mind." In his analysis, there are two types of investors, each with a different mindset: those who go for the packaged investment, and those who customize investments to suit their objectives.

- The need to work to learn and not to work for money

The reader of Rich Dad Poor Dad is given an example of a young woman who had a Master's Degree in English Literature and who was offended when it was suggested that she learns to sell and do direct marketing. After all the hard work for her degree, she didn't think she would have to stoop so low to learn how to be a salesperson, a profession she didn't think very highly of. The author uses this example to emphasize that there are other skills people need to cultivate to help them on the road towards financial freedom. Kiyosaki mentions management skills. He says individuals need to know how to manage cash flow, systems, and people. To that he throws in selling and marketing skills. He puts equal emphasis on communication skills. He says there are many people who have the scientific bent and hence have a powerhouse of knowledge, but they fail miserably in communications. These are the people who are "one skill away from great wealth." Kiyosaki suggested that one of the first and most important lessons he learned was to get out of the "Rat Race", instead of spending your life working to put a little money in your pocket and a bunch of money in someone else's pocket, have people work hard to put money in your pocket. Owning a business is the best and fastest way to earn big and a sure way to becoming rich.

Robert Kiyosaki's great work and suggestions on how to become financially independent rhymes well with thousands of others but you will notice small but very important nuances with other authors and motivational speakers. Kiyosaki's suggestions were very well received by the public and experts alike, his book because a best seller and a reference for hundreds of other works as is the case for our book now. However the suggestion made that the rich hardly pay tax should not be construed as a suggestion not to pay or avoiding paying taxes. Despite not always agreeing, feeling and seeing the work of government, we should pay our share of taxes as government is the guaranty of fair play for institutions that will hold or handle your wealth. All during your efforts in building wealth, they create the environment and set the rules to protect you from abuse. Besides the rich's down fall often comes in the form of tax audit or IRS prosecution for tax evasion, there are thousands of rich people who downgraded social classes to end up in the middle class after tax audits. It's very important to get very good education on how to get rich and being inspired by people how inspire the world, when it comes to motivational speaking or wealth building.

The advantage of information that is based on experience and years of study is that it is tried and tested and you can easily adapt it to your situation or context and put it to work for you with a higher probability of success. To Get rich truly has become easy as opportunities are all around us and there are needs unfulfilled that result in business opportunities and creating or tapping into different revenue streams has become easy in our day and age with various financial products in the market. This book makes a suggestion on how to get rich quick and build wealth, the suggestion is based on building a positive mental attitude, one were we feel rich before getting there and take specific steps to earn and grow money. Your mental attitude and personality is highly emphasized in the works of Katherine Hurst, a motivational speaker and author of several books. Katherine Hurst is another that inspired us in this book and we will look at her key suggestions when it comes to creating wealth. Katherine Hurst runs the largest law of attraction based motivational education in the world and she suggests that if you have a scarcity state of mind (poor man's mentality), it would be best to have a rich person's mentality. According to Katherine Hurst's Law of Attraction, your thoughts give rise to your reality. Therefore, if you think in ways that fuel a lifestyle that lacks financial security, you will continue to need more money, stay in the grip of poverty. There again, if you develop positive thought patterns, with positive intentions, with purposeful and deliberate action, you can vastly improve your wealth building financial journey.

Katherine Hurst makes 4 powerful inspirational suggestions:

- Perspective

If you imagine that most people are wealthier than you are then you are probably wrong. In order to magnetize the abundance of wealth, you need to shift your mindset so that you no longer feel poor. One way to achieve your aim is to gain perspective. Change your attitude about money by becoming grateful for the finances that you have right now. You might not be able to buy some of the things you want right now, but do not focus on such matters. Instead of concentrating on your present lack, appreciate your approaching gains.

- Examine your beliefs about money

Countless negative sayings about money become the mantras of people who practice scarcity thinking. Sure, money does not literally grow on trees, but keep telling yourself that it doesn't and you will be convinced that it is in short supply. Likewise, if you believe that money is the root of all evil, your ambition to gain wealth will conflict with your view that financial prosperity relates to immorality. Your negative thoughts about money will block wealth from coming your way. Katherine Hurst suggests that you develop new, positive beliefs about money and remind yourself about them regularly. For instance, tell yourself that you are just as capable of obtaining wealth as countless millionaires who made their fortunes. The only difference between you and rich people, is simply mindset. Now that you are developing a rich person mentality, you are starting to think like a millionaire, and your thoughts will influence the lifestyle that you want. Additionally, create positive sayings about wealth such as, "money provides freedom," and "the more money I have, the more people I can provide with financial assistance." Repeat the sentences that you develop several times a day and you will automatically drop negative thoughts about money, such as the idea that only mean people are rich.

- Use brain training audio programs

Katherine Hurst advises that there are a few really good audio programs designed to empower your brain to think faster, clearer and become more focused, enabling you to achieve any goal you put your mind to with ease. You can literally 'program' your brain for success and flip on that switch that will give you a rich person's mentality.

- Share Your Wealth

You might think that you need to keep hold of your money in order to become more prosperous. However, people with a rich person mentality never feel so poor that they are unable to spread a little of their abundance. In fact, many wealthy people give 10% of their money away to charities. You do not need to follow suit, but you can drop coins in a donation box, or give something away, when you feel a scarcity mentality looming.

"Your thoughts give rise to your reality!!!" This should be one of the most powerful quotes to retain in this chapter for you can get rich right now by simply changing your thinking. Finally to get rich quick is to quickly get yourself to think or have a wealth mentality commonly found in rich people. If you want prosperity, change your thoughts so that they mimic those of the super-rich. Ditch negative beliefs and sayings about money in favor of more sensible thoughts. Furthermore, do not be afraid to share your wealth. The result will be that you open your mind so that you are ready to receive financial rewards. It's easy to see the difference between Robert T. Kiyosaki and Katherine Hurst suggestions but in the end the same suggestion comes back again and again, the fact that to get rich you need to have a rich mentality, have a different perspective about money and be fearless, adventurous when it comes to earning money and always take action. Brian Tracy is another world renowned motivational speaker whose suggestions we will review now but we have to mention the fact that there are literally hundreds of motivational speakers of wealth and wealth building around the world and you can't possibly follow all of them as sometime they have conflicting suggestions. You will however notice that the three inspiring authors we mentioned, they have about the same suggestions although the approaches are different.

Brian Tracy suggests that we need to change our thinking and observe 5 mentality shifts wealthy people lived by to achieve financial freedom.

"One of the most important responsibilities you have to yourself and your loved ones is for you to achieve your own financial freedom over the course of your working lifetime." Brian Tracy. In order to achieve financial freedom, it is absolutely essential that you change your thinking in several specific ways. Financial freedom is terribly important to you, for every part of your life, including even how long you live.

- The first mental shift is from financial freedom by accident to financial freedom by design.

Financial freedom must be the center piece of all your work and external activities. It must be something that you specifically think about, define, and plan for continuously. Today, just as you design your dream house, you must design your financial future. You must think long term, many years down the road, and make an absolutely clear decision that you are going to achieve specific financial goals on a time table, year by year until you reach the point where you never have to work again unless you want to.

- Another mental shift you have to make in achieving financial freedom is from a survival consciousness to a prosperity consciousness.

Most people are locked into a survival consciousness. They are worried, guarded and careful about money. Wealthy people think in terms of prosperity rather than survival. They move from limitation thinking to abundance thinking. Wealthy people look upon the world around them as being full of opportunities to acquire and keep the money and they are constantly looking for ways to do it. They look at every new product and process, every technological market or breakthrough, as a possible opportunity to prosper in some way. Instead of thinking about how little they have, wealthy people are thinking about how much they want to acquire.

- Another shift in thinking is from security thoughts to opportunity thoughts.

You don't achieve financial freedom by playing it safe. You become financially independent by leading the field. This doesn't mean that you risk your money or throw it around. It means that you are willing to move out of your comfort zone and to try something new and different before everyone else starts trying or doing it. I have met countless salespeople and businessmen around the country who changed their entire lives by recognizing an opportunity and taking action on it before the vast majority of people woke up to it. By the time the dust had settled they were well established and had made more money in three or four years than they might have made in 30 or 40 years doing something else in an established field.

- Another mental shift you must make to achieve financial freedom is to change your thinking from spending to saving.

W. Clement Stone said that, "If you cannot save money, the seeds of greatness are not in you." We grow up from a young age spending everything we can get our hands on and a little bit more besides. The average young married couple in America spends 110% of their income, making up the difference with credit and loans from their families. With this attitude and approach to life, especially when it becomes a habit, their ability to save, accumulate, and acquire wealth is almost zero. In study after study on financial independence, it is generally agreed by every expert that you have to save approximately 20% to 30% of your income if you want to finally reach the point where you have enough money so that you'd never have to worry about it again. The wonderful thing is that, once you begin saving more and more of your income off the top, and living on the rest, you will find that you experience no discomfort at all. You become quite comfortable living on a lesser amount.

- Financial accumulation requires you to change your thinking from wishing and hoping to thinking and doing.

Don't talk to anyone else about your plans and your activities. Begin to accumulate money quietly and confidentially. Once you begin putting it away, don't ever let anyone know how much you have. Refuse to engage about conversations about money or to tell anyone about your financial accumulation account. There is something about keeping your plans and processes secret that gives them strength and power and causes them to work even more effectively for you. You will find that wealthy people never talk to others about their money. They are extremely private. Wealthy people have learned over time that the more secretive they are, the more effective they seem to be in acquiring and keeping ever greater amounts of money.

Brian Tracy finally suggests that the road to financial freedom is and has always been the miracle of compound interest. When you begin putting money away and then investing it carefully to build a financial estate, the miracle of compound interest clicks in. As you begin to move toward financial freedom, slowly at first, but then faster and faster as the years pass, you will feel absolutely wonderful about yourself.

It was important to share in this book the works of these three successful and wealthy authors on wealth building who contributed to the inspiration of this book, in fact based on our observations and for continuous education on how to get rich and stay rich reading their works will be great education and motivation for your objectives; Getting Rich. Everyone needs to be inspired in everything they do, in this world there are millions of millionaires and most certainly one that has a very similar background to yours. Studying or taking them as models will help you further in your journey to creating, growing and maintaining your wealth. Obviously you need to remove any limitations you may have placed on yourself consciously or unconsciously, anyone can start a business, anyone can achieve millionaire status, anyone can get out of the modern day exploitative slavery and anyone can get Rich Quick.

The wealth in this world is owned by only a few people, an estimated 1% of the earth population owned 90% of the wealth in the world and that includes all the privileges that come with having such wealth that is; control of governments, banking institutions, legislation, military, societies etc..... The 1% pretty much sets up the tempo for the average person's life from how much interest you will pay at the bank to what you will eat, drink, how you will live, play and even love. The system is set up so that the average person works to support it, you will earn just enough to keep you going. The average joe when it comes to wealth and money pay for everything in our society, the government takes a cut on everyone's pay and it needs to keep everyone working and paying to sustain itself; the people pay for everything you can imagine, from every disaster to government services. So much is done to keep people down, the system is not built to produce millionaires instantly because who will be left to do the work?

This book is so important that reading and applying the suggested methods of getting rich and building wealth will allow you to take the short cut to financial independence. This book reveals the secret to getting rich there is nothing else, that is the secret and taking it accepting it and applying it to change your life will allow you to be free, financially free, and morally free, free for the daily chains of modern day exploitative slavery; out of the daily race for money. Focus and concentrate on making money and attracting money because everything else is a distraction to keep you from acquiring wealth. There is an infinite amount of money in the world as wealth keeps expending every second, there will never be a shortage of wealth and when we say wealth we do not only refer to paper money but everything that constitute part of values in this world; properties, precious metals, stocks, bonds, mutual funds, business, etc……

Again being rich is having money, enough money to satisfy all your wants and needs while being wealthy is not only having money, enough money and assets to satisfy all your wants and needs but also heaving a wealth mentality. Getting to a wealth mentality quickly is to Get Rich Quick.

Get Rich Quick Build Wealth Now

Chapter II

Build Wealth Now

Build Wealth Now in this book's context means adopting immediately the habits and behaviors that are conducive to wealth building. The previous chapter has pretty much taught you what to do to have a wealth mentality and that building wealth requires specific knowledge from the way money works to accounting to entrepreneurial skills. Our suggestion will be to read Chapter 1 twice before moving on to insure that you fully absorb and understand. Chapters 1 and 2 are very critical to understand the book and the suggested method of getting and building wealth so reading attentively and perhaps even taking notes will greatly help you get the most out of this book. The easiest way to understand any concept is often through practical examples and short anecdotes. We have used a lot of works from various authors to illustrate certain points that are critical in your objective of getting rich and building wealth. This chapter 2 will make suggestions on how to build wealth and maintain it because it's not enough to have a wealth mentality, you need to keep the wealth you create and grow it.

Throughout this book we will emphasize the fact that modelling or emulating those who are doing better than we are or those who are where we want to be is the best way to getting to wealth. Grant Cardone is a highly successful entrepreneur, New York Times best-selling author, and sales training expert, a self-made millionaire fitting in the category of most people who had to work and actually build their wealth from scratch. There is something important to learn from Mr. Cardone, a down to earth self-made man who speaks in simple terms in an interview with American cnbc.com as he makes the following suggestions to those working to build wealth; Grant Cardone says *"Too many people out there are offering ridiculous ideas on how you can become rich. I can promise you that you will not get rich by skipping your daily latte. Look, if you don't have income then there is no money to save. Don't let anyone give you the idea that you need to skip your little pleasure and save $3 a day and that will somehow turn into a fortune. If you can skip your daily pleasure be it a drink or else costing you $5 every day and save $10,000 over the next five years, but if you think $10,000 is going to change your life, you're not just broke, you're being stupid. Of course you should spend less than you earn, but if you* make $50,000 a year with a couple of kids, what money is there left over to save?"

Grant Cardone suggests that if you are serious about getting rich, you need to get your mind focused on income. Increase your income enough and you will be able to save something substantial. The following tips will actually get you to millionaire status:

Invest in you; Successful people invest time, energy, and money in improving themselves. A man told me once, "The best way you can help people in need is to not be someone in need." This means investing in yourself to become great at something. I invested in sales training when I was 25. That made my income-producing ability skyrocket. Investing in yourself is the best investment you can make.

Find a job in the right vehicle; the rich are able to get in with the right company where there is opportunity for growth. My VP of sales Jarrod Glandt started working for me over seven years ago for $2,500 a month. He wasn't making anything but he was in the right vehicle. He grew his skill set and was able to multiply his monthly income many times over because he knew I was looking to expand. Too many people just look for a job. You need a job, but you need the right vehicle. All companies live from this thing called revenue. Get commissions rather than just a salary and you will finally be in control of how much you earn.

Get great at what you do; Commit to being great, not just average. Any industry can be a painful profession for average and bottom performers, but massively rewarding for those that are great. Those that live, breathe, and eat their profession, those that are obsessed, become great.

I have never met a great who wasn't all in and completely consumed by their trade. Have you?

The fact is, if you aren't great, you are average. The rich get great.

Get multiple, connected income streams flowing; you won't get rich without multiple flows of income. That starts with the income you currently have. Increase that income and start adding multiple flows. You want what are called symbiotic flows. Do not just add disconnected flows. Instead, find other ways you can add income to the job you already have.

Hit $100K, then invest the rest; first, try to save $100,000 or any other significant amount for your level of income. Why? You need to prove to yourself that you can go out and get money. If you only have $10,000 saved, your only priority should be increasing your income so that you can save more. Saving $100,000 shows that you have an ability to make money and then to keep it. Most people can't do either of those things.

Once you can earn and save, then you can start building wealth. I'd recommend multi-family real estate if you are conservative like me. I never looked to get rich quick, but I did look to get rich.

Grant Cardone provides absolutely important suggestions for anyone looking to grow wealth and that's to have an income, increase income or have the ability to increase income and if you are working it's either through commissions, bonuses, incentives or anything you have control over. For anyone working therefore having a source of income increasing your income is a must let's remember that poverty is chasing everyone irrespective of your status in society. Government workers may have some restrictions and its best to investigate with the public service commission or your HR department what sort of side business or occupation could be restricted before taking on any business. When working on a salary you are boxed into a pay that limits you and your ability to get rich quick and build wealth now. Generating various sources of revenues while earning an income is best, passive income can be earned through the financial markets investing in shares, bonds, mutual funds or simply investing in a startup company. To build wealth really fast, investing in a retirement fund will not get you there especially because come retirement you may not be able to enjoy your money as you could in your 40s or 50s. While investing $50 to $100 every month into a retirement fund could be a great long-term strategy, it's not going to make a difference in the short-term. Building wealth will require that you work with a financial adviser because knowing where you want to be it's certainly better if your financial advisor gives you a variety of options based on your financial goals. It's always a good idea to talk to several professional financial advisors and investors to see what has worked for them. As you make it a habit to find ways to better yourself and increase your income, you'll also find new potential ways to build wealth faster than ever, keep your ears and eyes open to see new opportunities to earn extra income. Everyone does it differently, and nobody will do it exactly like you because your circumstances are different, building wealth is a topic that sparks heated debate, promotes quirky "get rich quick" schemes and leading people to investment avenues or transactions they might otherwise never consider. For most of us, getting rich seems like an elusive concept that can feel far off and unattainable especially with the mounting costs of living in most countries around the world. But the reality is that no matter your financial circumstances; age, education, physical handicap, you can build wealth by observing certain steps recommended by those who took them before you and succeeded. No matter where you stand today you can build wealth and get rich with simple deliberate moves planning and discipline. You will not get rich through keeping money in a savings account, which should only be a parking place for your money while waiting to invest or put it to work elsewhere.

Getting rich, building wealth all comes down to accumulating money over time, managing it a certain way and adopting behaviors that allow you to keep what you have earned;

Earn money. You have to have income, a source of revenues. You cannot become rich or build wealth without earning money, you need to insure that you continuously earn money be it a salary or passive income, through rentals, investments or a business. There are two types of income earned (salary, commissions) basically anything you offered a service or time in exchange for money and passive income (income which derived from investments). Do not underestimate the earning potential of useful well located micro businesses, many billionaires come from micro businesses.

Save when you earned. Having an income will allow you to meet your daily needs and wants; with the extra money left, saved you can start building wealth. The small island of Japan is well known for having the highest rate of its population saving part of their income. Japan was the 2nd largest economy in the world for decades as they had a culture of innovation and savings. In contrast we live in a country were very often people spend 100% of what they have earned. Saving also means spending carefully and not leaving above and beyond your earning ability. If your wants and needs exceed your income saving becomes impossible therefore achieving wealth realistic. Taking control over your earnings and spending may require that you develop a budget and stick to it. Give into your needs and not so much into your wants if you are to succeed in saving money.

Grow your savings. Having money saved will open new doors for you to invest to grow your money, investing will allow you to grow your money faster to reach your target. Growing your wealth means learning best practice and looking out for opportunities, you will notice that reaching a certain level of income will lead to more comfort and you will keep getting richer and richer. Money will come to you much easier than before. Diversification will be key in your youth and less so as you go passed the age of 45 when you may not be able to tolerate higher risk profile investments. Investing in real estate is great as it preserves your money and grows as the property grows in value, exposure to the financial markets is another way to grow your money, investment vehicles such as mutual funds, bonds fixed-income exposures are perfect as part of diversification of your investment. You may live in a country where some investment vehicles widely available elsewhere are not accessible. You can always open a foreign account in most countries to take advantage of these wealth building products and services. Investing in bricks and mortar small companies may be a better option for you in case you can't access other types of investment vehicles. If you have read about Africa's richest man Aliko Dangote then you will know that his wealth came from direct investments in strategic (staple) businesses.

The basic easy math to build wealth is:

Income - Spending = Savings + Investment = Wealth

Attaining the status of being wealthy will obviously depend on a lot of factors; where you live, how you live, your family obligations, your education, how you spend your money. Having a million US dollars may not be enough for a US citizen to feel wealthy whereas having a million US dollars to a Cameroonian Citizen certifies him as a wealthy person because it represents 550,000,000 five hundred and fifty millions CFA Francs in their currency, in a country where minimum wage can be as low as 40,000 CFA Francs per month that is close to 73 US dollars. In the US you can never pay anyone 73 US dollars per month even for domestic work, you will even get arrested for paying bellow the federal minimum wage.

So to build wealth you have to takes steps necessary to reach the status of being rich based on where you live first and go on to reach a global status of wealth after. We have no choice but to depend on money and wealth creation to survive, without money we cannot do anything in fact we are nothing without money no matter where in the world you live. Money is not just the paper kind, it can be anything that represents currency anywhere around the world because elsewhere wealth is expressed in what you own unfortunately or fortunately depending how you have come to see it, money is a necessary evil. But just be careful how you look at money from what you should have learned so far in the previous chapter, money is to be respected and should not be looked at as anything negative in our life. We spend most of our time concerned with money worried that we may not have enough. Getting rich quick in the context of waking up to having money is not realistic and that kind of money does not last long, lottery or inheritance may not be good for you unless you have prepared to receive it. Sudden wealth very often dramatically changes people's lives for the best temporarily and if not managed well which is the case for many who received sudden wealth the end up in the grips of poverty. Ideally it should take time and a lot of work to build wealth. This book should be one in many other steps you take to prepare for creating, growing and saving wealth to get rich. Everyone wants to get rich quick, now but they forget the work needed to get there, it's an adventure, a game with rules to respect and only when you respect the rules you make it. As part of anyone's strategy to getting rich investing is part of it as well as savings, While there is a limit to how much you can save as in spend less, there is never a limit on your earning potential. As you start to invest your mortal enemy should be inflation as it works against your purchasing power and the value of your money over time meaning you could be saving for 10 years and if you did not beat inflation your money would not have grown in fact would be worth less than when you place it in savings, you would not be able to buy the same thing you could buy with such an amount 10 years earlier. We live in a capitalist society, a consumer's world, a world where the more poor people the better for some, that's why in all countries around the world 1 to 20 % of the population usually own 80 to 99 % of the country's wealth. People through their businesses device daily means to get you to spend your money on them, you probably have bought things that turned out to be useless over time when in fact when you bought it seemed like a great idea. Look around your home and ask yourself if you absolutely need all that stuff you have around you. You will realize that you need to spend on what is absolutely necessary and avoid wasting money.

"Wealth gained hastily will dwindle, but whoever gathers little by little will increase it."- Proverbs 13:11

Building wealth is not something you will just stumble upon one day. It's something you work at every day, forever. Our time is different and we need to adapt to our circumstance today because today money keeps the world spinning. We have to strongly reject the millennia suggested notion of money being the root of all evil and that money is not everything; money is everything, money is the source of happiness and in our world being poor is a sin. In today's society being poor is a sin, you don't contribute to society and you can't help your own family if you are poor, hell you can't even pay your tithes to your church, synagogue or mosque. We can no longer afford not to act to get out of poverty and be financially independent knowing what is at stake; your freedom. Without money you will fall prey to people and be subjected to their will, we work daily to make money, getting our money to work hard for us limits our need to work as hard.

Build wealth because your life depends on it, build wealth to protect yourself and the ones you love, build wealth because it gives you power, build wealth because it is power, true power for it solves all sorts of problems in our society. Because wealth will change you it requires adopting a certain behavior. You have probably heard the saying that goes "absolute power corrupts absolutely" well because wealth is power, wealth will change you and the change can be positive or negative on your character and people around you will notice the change. A quick but slow accumulation of wealth will help you adapt to the change as you grow. This is only natural because looking at ourselves as humans we gain access to certain privileges only as we grow older because only at certain ages can we handle the consequences brought on by those; such as alcohol, sex, voting, signatory powers etc.… we now know that having money and wealth is and requires a specific state of mind. Your consciousness will determine your being and state of wealth accumulation because you will either attract wealth or repel it with your thoughts. To accumulate wealth get into that state of mind that attract money, work or put systems in place to earn money, the more you earn the better, develop various ways to generate money. Beyond earning money and saving money to invest, financial literacy has been emphasized throughout this book therefore learning to earn, save and invest should be part of your overall strategy to Build Wealth Now.

Get Rich Quick Build Wealth Now

Chapter III

The Pursuit of Happiness

The Pursuit of Happiness, perhaps you have seen the movie, featuring Will Smith and his son Jaden Smith? The movie is very inspiring, powerful and moving. If you have not seen it, it's basically a biography of a man who struggled to attain a level of comfort in his life. The lack of money and the continuous daily struggle to meet their needs was the main reason behind his separation from his wife and mother of his son. Having moved on, leaving the main character of the movie, he was left to raise his son alone, he had no money, no home, no job and depended on hand outs, homeless shelters and soup kitchens to satisfy his and his son's basic needs. Despite the hardship the man was determined to succeed and refused to be a basket case, he took additional classes acquired new skills and make enormous sacrifices to rise out of the grip of poverty. The movie strongly suggests that money or wealth in today's society has become an imperative factor for happiness, lack of money is a source of a lot of hardship and misery. No one should live in poverty but it does not mean that being poor dooms you to unhappiness for life. We suggest that seeking wealth is factually trying to get the assurance of happiness and comfort. It's often said money can't buy you happiness but that saying is mostly philosophical and no longer represents our current society.

Happiness is not a permanent feeling as it comes and goes, you can feel happy now and be unhappy an hour later, no one can ever be in a permanent state of happiness. There are arguments that happiness is a state of mind and cannot be pursued or attained because of material things like homes, cars, jewelry etc.....

There are many arguments against basing your happiness on your successful pursuit of wealth and we owe it to the reader to present the other people's case against the material based pursuit of happiness.

A very successful and wealthy Psychologist Leon F. Seltzer, Ph.D., a clinical psychologist and the author of Paradoxical Strategies in

Psychotherapy, a holder of doctorates in English and Psychology; made the suggestions bellow pertaining to seeking wealth as a way to insure happiness. You have to remember that happiness is a state of mind you can be happy with or without money but Get Rich Quick, Build Wealth now suggests that Being Rich is Better than being poor and people like this wealthy Psychologist should not prevent you from building wealth or surrounding yourself with things that will contribute to your happiness. The good doctor makes the following statements in an article in Psychology today's website. "Once you experience contentment (*not* complacence) with your lot in life, neither financial assets nor physical robustness are pivotal to such well-being. Your peace of mind, your overarching satisfaction with your existence (despite its inevitable ups-and-downs) is secured. So the calmness and cheer of what's going on inside your head (i.e., the "buoyancy" of your thoughts and feelings) far eclipse the turmoil, the gloom and doom that may be taking place outside.

And in your general acceptance of life you gain ultimate control over it. However much you might wish to see positive changes in the world, to bear witness to the betterment of humankind and society, you also accept that your ability to influence external events is limited. You do what you can, but you don't anguish over the current state of affairs, or about the unalterable framework of mortal existence. What *is* is good enough for you.

Moreover, happiness as an enduring state of mind is (at least potentially) available at any time. It doesn't need to be pursued (as, say, a luxury sports car, a bracelet from Tiffany's, or tickets to the Super Bowl). It's nothing that requires questing after since, once you've come to wholly embrace yourself and the world around you, it already exists safely inside you. In fully espousing the world with all its inequities, injustices, and suffering your happiness is removed from harm's way.

Achieving such a state of acceptance, or being, is really the ultimate "gift" to yourself. And again, it's not anything that requires being hunted down from the outside then somehow "assimilated" from within.

On the contrary, chasing happiness through the acquisition of wealth, through amassing more and more things, is a fool's pursuit. For once such material appetites are aroused, at a certain point they become insatiable. Substituted for longer-term satisfactions, the pleasures and gratifications they yield are more or less fleeting. In addition, no amount of money can suffice when sooner or later fortune-seeking itself has become obsessive.

When that critical line is crossed, the pursuit is no longer a means to some presumably fulfilling end. It is the end.

And once, paradoxically, the goal has become the pursuit of the goal you're left in the self-defeating position of hunting down that which can never be captured. Like an unquenchable thirst, not the riches but the lust for riches can never be satisfied. Materialistically searching for happiness through accumulating wealth invariably cries out for more of the same.

This incessant seeking for what can never be definitively achieved explains why many millionaires and especially, billionaires can be so aggressive, so merciless, in their ongoing exploits to accrue more wealth. Addictively chasing incalculable riches, a fortune going far beyond the dreams of avarice (as though such a radical pursuit must somehow vindicate their self-interested "cause"), they end up monomaniacal, megalomaniacal, inhuman and to say the least inhumane.

Their bullheaded endeavors become ever more competitive, mercenary, ruthless, and mean-spirited. Consider, for example, the billionaire Koch brothers and their latest underhanded but unmitigated efforts at busting unions, which stand in the way of their amassing yet even greater profits. Just as addicts typically require increasingly more of their "drug of choice" to get high, those who are already wealthy need ever greater wealth to feel employing a phrase I regard as crucial "good enough". And because, as the philosopher Eric Hoffer put it, "You can never get enough of what you don't really want," the key to lasting happiness is never accessible to them.

Having worked professionally with several multimillionaire malcontents, I can say that what they really craved were those things intrinsic to happiness laid out at the beginning of this post. The transient highs that accompanied their wealth accumulation were never much more than a hormonal rush anyway. And even though in the eyes of the world they were enormously successful, continuing frustrations and insecurities gave testimony to the fact that the blast of "feel good" chemicals their success yielded was all too easily exhausted.

Money can't buy harmonious, fulfilling relationships with others. And it certainly doesn't have the power to generate unconditional acceptance of self. For such an internal embrace bears little connection to your bank account. In fact, your monetary wealth, so far from securing this single most important relationship in your life, ends up making it all the more conditional. As long as you measure your self-worth in dollars and cents, it must rise or fall in accordance with the success (or failure) of your latest enterprise.

Moreover, people with extreme wealth tend to be tight-fisted, almost miserly. Statistics repeatedly show that the very rich donate disproportionately less to charitable organizations than do members of the middle class. And how could this be otherwise when contributing substantial sums of money to worthy causes cannot but be experienced by them as reducing their personal worth--which they've learned to appraise financially. However unconsciously, actually giving money *away* is precarious to their (monetarily-based) self-image.

At last, compulsive efforts to somehow "purchase" happiness is akin to reaching out toward a greased object that, even if momentarily snatched, is downright impossible to hold onto. Similarly, worshiping the false god of Mammon enslaves you to objects of desire that can never be held fast. Even when they do appear caught, they offer only temporary highs . . . never happiness. Still, seduced by what our society typically defines as success (watch enough TV commercials and you'll get an acute sense of how success is portrayed in the media), it's easy enough to lose your way and zealously embark on a path incapable of providing any real sustenance.

So, obsessively questing after wealth and all that it can buy ultimately sows the seeds of later frustration and disappointment. If your appetite for riches, or a super-luxurious lifestyle, is now threatening to become addictive, you may wish to reconsider whether pursuing such affluence is really a worthy goal. Remember, inevitably you have to "come down" from what, frankly, may be a terrific high. But if, instead, you devote yourself to becoming high on life or rather, give up getting high for truly getting happy a far more lasting state of well-being may await you."

End of quote and we could not disagree more with this wealthy good doctor; we concede that you have different sources of happiness which can derive from materials or spiritually. It is a fact that a dirt poor person can feel moments of happiness and that a super-rich person can have moments of unhappiness but to condemn the rich to possibly an artificial happiness is being dishonest. The pursuit of happiness and seeking wealth has been viewed as being one in the same by most people as having wealth opens so many doors and provide you with better possibilities or more frequent moments of happiness. Our society automatically associates wealth with happiness and we suggest that those two have become imperatively associated whenever anyone claims to be happy. In this book we suggest that seeking to build wealth is indeed the pursuit of happiness but we emphasis having a wealth mentality so that one has a balanced view of life to avoid having your money make you unhappy. We also understand that if happiness is conceived in monetary terms, then the more money or assets you acquire, the happier you should be but unfortunately the materialistically pursuing happiness cannot stand alone in making you happy as you could amass wealth and be unhappy because of your wealth. We advocate a balanced mind and behavior towards wealth and wealth acquisition relating to happiness.

The spiritual perspective of happiness will obviously be easier to attain because it's born out of psychological conditioning. If you believe you are happy then you are happy but if you do not think you are happy than you are not happy. Leon F. Seltzer, Ph.D., in his article against the pursuit of happiness through material things made clear his preference for the spiritual aspect of Happiness. Seltzer makes this suggestion; "By "spiritual," I'm envisioning this ideal state as emanating from a variety of non-materialistic attainments. Which would include a fulfilling sense of belonging or community with others and all of nature; the development of warm, supportive, mutually self-disclosing relationships; an unconditional love, respect, and acceptance of self-one that's totally independent of environmental circumstances; and an almost unassailable state of well-being (having little to do with personal health, and even less.

But wealth or money in today's world is a problem solver at all levels of society everywhere in our lives. People will love you because of money, you can cure yourself of most ailments thanks to money, your life expectancy increases when you have money, if you don't like your looks you can change, there are so many advantages money provides including the ability to spread joy and help others in need. Believe that money can make you or significantly contribute to making you happy. Try living without money or with very little money and you will come to see life differently, hard and unpleasant. In looking to be rich we are in fact in pursuit of happiness and of course having money is not all you need to be happy just like you can't really be happy in our time without money. Having money will give you in this time and life several advantages; we live in systems that could see us die because we do not have money to pay for medication, we won't even mention the need to feed ourselves, need for shelter etc.....

Several countries around the world have placed the pursuit of happiness as part of inalienable right and nature of people. Looking into the definition of pursuit of happiness to understand why we aspire to be rich we will look into the reason for example why the founding fathers of the United States included the pursuit of happiness in the constitution in drafting the declaration of independence.

Let's look at the definition of happiness and pursuit of happiness, various sources have study or search of the meaning of both the psychological and philosophical pursuit of happiness beginning in China, India and Greece nearly 2,500 years ago with Confucius, Buddha, Socrates, and Aristotle. There are a lot of similarities between these thinkers in their time and scientists of our time who are spending a lot of time trying to define the pursuit of happiness. There are several scientific studies on Positive Psychology and the science of happiness. We believe what makes happy people happy has been discovered. These scientific studies point to specific ways of thinking and acting that can strongly impact our personal sense of happiness and peace of mind. The resulting scientific discoveries are enriching the practices of counseling, clinical psychology, psychiatry and life coaching. It's been discovered that people who have one or more close relationships that is friendships are happier. People who volunteer or simply care for others on a consistent basis seem to be happier and less depressed. Regular exercise has been associated with improved mental well-being and a lower incidence of depression. Exercise has a large clinical impact on depression and level of happiness.

In trying to reach a personal goal, being well trained and working with ease allow us to fill happy. According to Mihaly Csikszentmihalyi, a pioneer of the scientific study of happiness, *flow* is a type of intrinsic motivation. Many kinds of activities, such as sports, playing an instrument, or teaching, can produce the experience of flow. In his words, "you do what you're doing primarily because you like what you're doing. If you learn only for external, extrinsic reasons, you will probably forget it as soon as you are no longer forced to remember what you want to do. Who ever said God or religion had nothing to do with happiness was wrong as it's been discovered and demonstrated that there is a close link between spiritual and religious practice and happiness. In studying people considered happy the happiest people are those that have discovered their unique strengths (such as persistence and critical thinking) and virtues (such as humanity) and use those strengths and virtues for a purpose that is greater than their own personal goals. Of all the areas studied in the relatively young field of positive psychology, gratitude has perhaps received the most attention. Grateful people have been shown to have greater positive emotion, a greater sense of belonging, and lower incidence of depression and stress.

Now having looked at how happiness is scientifically described and perceived or attainment of wellbeing today suggested, we have to keep in mind that a person poor or rich can feel happy. Every year Americans as do other people around the world celebrate the nation's Declaration of Independence and their constitutions which recognize that all men are "endowed by their creator with certain unalienable Rights, that among these are Life, Liberty and the pursuit of Happiness." Those words give a lot of importance to the Pursuit of happiness which we look into in this book with the firm believe that human rights are grounded in nature and the suggestion that the pursuit of happiness can only be properly understood from the perspective of natural law. The natural law insists that rights are grounded in the reality of human nature. Human nature is a universal and unchanging reality which remains the same all over the world and throughout history. Aristotle argues that life is the being of living things; that is, the very existence of animate beings is tied up with life. The powers of life, which in man includes the powers of reason and will, are caused by the presence of a soul, which is, as Aristotle says, the form of the body. Humans live so that they may attain happiness thus, humans have act in that most human way, to grow in wisdom and love.

There is a relationship between money and happiness or wealth and happiness but again happiness is a state of mind. But most people do not have the correct perception or mentality about money and its relationship with their state of mind or happiness. Looking at numbers to get an indication, in 2011, Americans carried $2.5 trillion in consumer debt (U.S. Federal Reserve). From 2000 to 2010 credit card use increased 50 percent (U.S. Census Bureau) and the average household has $10,678 in credit card debt (up 29 percent from 2000) while the personal savings rate have plummeted (U.S. Department of Commerce: Bureau of Economic Analysis, 2011). All the while the economy has been slow to recover from a housing crisis muddled with foreclosures and unemployment. People make us of more money to keep their lifestyles. Data collected at Beyond the Purchase suggest that while many Americans are in a state of financial crisis, their debt levels climbing as a result of poor money management and detrimental consumption behaviors, individuals who manage and track their expenses: (1) report more money in savings and investments, (2) carry lower credit card balances, and (3) have fewer maxed-out credit cards. All of these relations were significant even after controlling for important variables. That suggest that money management is the strongest predictor of wealth accumulation and debt reduction, even when holding age, personality, and materialism constant.

And the benefits of building wealth or better management of money go on. As individuals manage their money they report more life satisfaction, partly, it seems, because they feel more financially secure from their diligent money management. Understanding the relationship between money and happiness is knowing what might be influencing how you spend your money. With that information, you can better understand the ways in which your financial decisions affect your happiness. That is, since the goal of human existence lies in the exercise of reason and will, we have to be able to develop our intellect by growing in knowledge of truth and to perfect the will's love of the good by delighting in the goodness of creation, wealth thus the Pursuit of Happiness. In today's society we can't imagine a sustained state of happiness without access to money.

There will always be a debate on whether money can buy happiness or make you happy but the truth is that money makes it possible for you to have a roof over your head, put food on your plate and go out with your friends and family; have that quality time and build great memories. But they question you can ask yourself is which of these things actually makes you happy? Or when can money buy happiness for you? Well the answer is that yes in reality having more money does not result in more happiness. Research has repeatedly shown that once you reach a certain comfortable level of income that covers your basic needs; shelter, food, water, electricity etc....., having a higher income does not bring you more happiness. However, how you spend the extra disposable income that you do have left over after paying your bills does have an impact on your state of mind. If you can learn to spend this money right and you'll get the happiness boost you're looking for. Experts suggest that whenever making an acquisition, Buy experiences over objects. When you buy objects you tend to have a momentary happiness boost when you complete the purchase and perhaps the first time you use your new item. You quickly get used to owning it and stop feeling any excitement with it. Buy experiences and you'll get a triple happiness boost: when anticipating it in the future, when experiencing it in the present, and when reminiscing about it in the past. You're also much more likely to savor experiences rather than objects, connect with other people through them and get a deeper, more powerful positivity boost through all your five senses. Also save time and consider your time as precious because you'll never get time back once it's gone it's gone. Time is the one resource in this world that is the same for everyone. No one can buy it, create it or borrow it. No one can pause it, speed it up or change it. The only control you have over your time is how you spend it - and think wisely because you can never get it back. Usually it's worth paying 15% more to get a direct flight somewhere instead of a stopover that causes you stress and costs time. Sometimes it's better to stick to a job that's closer to home because the longer time you spend commuting, the more detrimental it is to your stress and happiness levels. Don't always sacrifice your time to save money - or even make more money. Think about what kind of use of your time is the likeliest to give you the least amount of stress and the most amount of happiness. Think about how you can make peace with time so that you feel more time affluent - as this is something that also naturally boosts your happiness. Even giving your time up for some volunteering can boost your happiness levels and improve your relationship with the clock. The pleasure of giving or the importance of thanksgiving is significant in contributing to making us happy.

Donating to a charity can have a happiness boost that is as powerful as doubling your household income. Choose acts of kindness and generosity that you're excited to do, and you'll feel even more connected to the cause. The more connected you are to how what you're donating is having a positive impact, the more impactful your happiness boost will be. It's also an opportunity for you to increase your sense of wealth as when you give money away you get a sense that you have so much that you can give away.

In 2017, on earth the foundation of happiness is money, wealth. The feeling may not depend on money but money is the cause, money makes it easier and possible. The happiest nations on earth are those considered wealthy, with economies that support and offer opportunities to a waste majority of its population. When gainfully employed and earning good money, one feels less stressed or depressed, more comfortable with the fact their wants and needs are met. We feel proud and honored when we can further help other people, make their lives better. Happiness whether it's in wealth or poverty it's a state of mind, it's not constant and perhaps since we are in control of our mood and happiness perhaps we don't need to be at the pursuit of happiness.

Get Rich Quick Build Wealth Now

Chapter IV
Dream Killers

Dream killers are everything that works to prevent you from being happy, reach your dreams and aspirations. Poverty is the ultimate dream killer. Poverty can be defined as lacking assets and money, being unable to satisfy your wants and daily needs. But poverty is a state of mind just as being rich and wealthy is a state of mind, money is in consciousness. In essence you can be your own ultimate dream killer what we mean by you is that your state of mind and attitude. In reality we are what we believe we are and we can make or break our own success. Composure and self-control is key to success because without self-control we will find ourselves incapable of a number of things. Dream killers are everywhere; its negative people, drugs, alcohol, your neighborhood, your job, your family responsibilities, your bad habits and so much more. It takes very little to undo years of hard work when it comes to having a balanced mind to build riches. The people closest to us can unconsciously kill our dreams and aspirations, the lack of trust from parents, family members, teachers and the society forces a person to drift away from their dreams and aspirations. The environment that creates doubts kills the aspirations of a human being, sometimes it's not self-doubt but it's the other people judging you, doubting you or demeaning you which gives you that uncomfortable feeling of doubt and ultimately abandon of your ambition. People who dare to think differently in our society face a lot of mistrust and are challenged not to prove their view points but to succumb to their doubts and dubiety. As a result our society is deprived of talent or the open field where everyone exercises their right to be successful or contribute to society in the best way they know how or can. That's is what has been called a glass ceiling effect for women as an example in the corporate world or black people in certain companies in America. Because of people's attitudes towards other people we lose creativity on a daily basis from people who give up on their dreams. We lose students who could have been potential biologists, doctors, physicist, pharmacist, writers, engineers, media persons and much more to apprehensiveness towards their aspirations. To be doubtful is something that is both a natural instinct and something inculcated in us by society. There will always be people who will judge a person from the way they see things because not everyone is capable of thinking out of the box. People tend to pull you down when they cannot or do not have your talent or strength and it is in that very moment that you need to embrace your spark, to trust your inner instincts. The intuition and the inner impulse is something that is proved to be right in majority of instances. Our sub-conscious mind somehow already knows that what a person is capable of; it knows when to take that one big leap, when to jump to the other side of the field where success awaits. But it requires willingness to reinforce the change and it definitely takes a lot of courage to go against the grain.

To overcoming obstacles that can kill your dreams Robert T. Kiyosaki's suggestion and experience is that five personality traits can hamper human beings in achieving their aspiration and he sites: fear, cynicism, laziness, bad habits, arrogance. These may seem like normal feelings that we can feel like fear as an example but the way we handle that fear is what makes the difference. Mister Kiyosaki shares his sentiment about his particular fondness for Texas and Texans: "When they win, they win big and when they lose, it's spectacular." Letting us understand that one should never fear to fail and should aspire for greatness perhaps beyond what we could have conceived.

Your journey to getting rich and building wealth has already started through a feeling or a dream, you have certainly felt or dreamed about being financially independent and having money in abundance. A dream be it at night or a day dream gave you aspirations to build wealth and that is the start, the first step you need to take to get wealthy. The pursuit of happiness is also another reason people want to get rich and build wealth; satisfy your needs and those of your loved ones, making them happy and keeping them save is an instinctive duty that makes us feel good when we succeed. We are happy to know we make people happy and safe, we have a sense of purpose in our lives when we know people depend on us and we fulfil the needs of our people. The dream killers are not limited to the personality traits mentioned above but insuring that you have the right attitude will allow you to beat dream killers. What we need to retain from this book is that your state of mind matters although Bloodline Entrapments are known kill dreams and limit people physically. Your mental state or environment can make you what you are so basically can make you or break you, being surrounded by positive and hardworking people will be a lot more advantageous than being surrounded by negative and lazy people. All of us know people who spend all their time complaining and being negative about everything, never living with hope. Some people just love to complain about everything and blame the system or else about their failures and inability to build wealth or achieve their goals. You should keep these types of people as far away from you as possible or keep your interaction with them very limited, we have so far learned that our state of mind can be subliminally programmed and keeping from bad habits will allow us to live to see our dreams realized.

Keeping away from negativity is very critical, we have learned about subliminal and neuro programming of our brain, what we need to understand is being around negative people or a negative environment will affect us whether we are conscious of it or not. Our brain is very powerful beyond our understanding and we only realize this when a person is put on hypnosis and while on that state can recall things in details, things he cannot recall normally. Under hypnosis we can remember things as far back as our childhood with accurate details. Anything we hear bellow 40 decibels goes directly in our subconscious and our brain may refer to it in our daily lives. Being exposed or hearing too many negative things can affect us in the long run, let's not hear negativity they are dream killers. Gossiping and negative news casts also contribute to a mental state of despair limiting your ability to think positive and dream big.

We should never be afraid of chasing your dreams, aspiration or experimenting because you will never know what the future holds or what the next moment possibly be unveiling if you are not willing to take that one chance. We should be unapologetic about being fearless and daring to explore the new ventures in life albeit not recklessly. You can drift apart from the crowd, blaze you own trail and wonder the unknown territory. Because mistrust from people, doubt or self-doubt impedes actions, you will never know what was meant to be yours, what you could have been, or what different your contribution to society could have been to the world meant to come from you. Self-doubt debars you from the liberty of innovation and limitless creativity. When aspiring to build wealth, long term plans are what leads to riches, generating income to meet one's daily needs and earning enough to have enough left to save and invest. We need to set goals daily if not hourly goals and work tirelessly to reach those, getting rich demands better organization, better management of our money and knowledge of financial management. When building wealth we also need to know that debt is the devil, or perhaps we should say not all debts are good especially because they do not come free of charge. While in debt, every dollar your earn or that comes to you is meant to return with another dollar, keeping you working harder to make money and making it difficult to save. Some debts are good in the sense that they allow you to acquire assets that can grow faster than the interest to be paid on the principal; real estate comes to mind, business loans also can be considered good debts, even the purchase of a new car if it leads to the ability to earn more. You will agree that having debt while trying to achieve financial independence is like trying to walk fast while facing a wind blowing at 100 km per hour.

While debt can be valuable and even profitable if used correctly, too many people spend money they don't have through consumer loans like local shop debts, store credit accounts, credit card loans, bank personal loans to name a few. The interest payable on those loans will keep you struggling and can even ruin you. No debt means no stress, means you are able to save and invest therefore build wealth. Anyone looking to get rich should first get rid of all their debts to see what they are worth. If you want to reach your dreams, making changes in your lifestyle can drastically improve your chances of achieving your objectives and life. If you are surrounded by friends who do not have financial independence as their goal or are irresponsible financially; true players for real who go out for entertainment all the time, spend uncontrollably on frivolous stuff, funny gadgets and unessential things. Reaching your targets of building wealth around such people will be much harder and trying to keep up with the super-rich like the Dangotes is futile because you are not at the same level of income or wealth and following the super-rich in their spending habits will not be in your favor. You want to surround yourself with people who have the same goals as you and people you can learn from.

Your job could be a dream killer for it will take your full time attention and leave very little time for you to look into other opportunities that could help you build your wealth. Certain jobs will keep you very busy leaving no time for anything else and letting you earn just enough to keep you going until your next pay check. You may have a great job with great pay but that will not get you rich unless you have profit sharing with the company or earn large enough bonuses based on your employer's performance. The best way to keep bumping your income higher than the 3% annual salary increase is to move from one company to another while in the same field every few years. When moving from one job to another, the salary offered can be as much as 30% of your current income, you obviously would have to move to a company that is stable, doing well. You must and should be able to negotiate your annual salary increase so you can beat the cost of living increase and monetary inflation. Your money loses value every second of every day through inflation and things get expensive because of the market economy; supply and demand. Raw materials can be of short supply driving the value added product's price higher or as labor costs increase the manufactured products increases in cost. This has the implication that the money you have or make today will not be able to buy the same items in the future at the same price. If you manage to make more money from your normal income or increased income, the extra cash earned can be invested in anything that will generate passive income. The best job that could almost guarantee that you will be rich is a merit based pay, commission based or performance based job. The majority of working people who became millionaires held merit or commission based jobs with bonuses, incentives, profit sharing and share options.

Your education or lack thereof can prevent you from attaining a certain level or position within your field of work closing doors to the extra income that you could get to build your riches. To grow you will have to upgrade your skills; you can take a class or read some books to gain more knowledge.

Behind any successful person there is a partner be it a business partner or a life partner, having someone you can count on on your journey to build wealth would be a boost and get you closer to your aspirations. Speaking of dream killers the wrong partner or being in the wrong relationship with someone who does not share or have the character traits needed to build wealth will surely stop you from achieving your goals. To achieve financial success or any sort of success in life one needs transformation a transition into another state of mind; a total life transformation won't happen overnight it takes time, work and this can happen at any time or age in our lives. We need to act on our dreams. Failure is what keeps us from taking that critical deciding leap in our lives. It is the fear of failure, which makes way for doubt to seep in and the voice of doubt generates uncertainty. Without the assurance that we will succeed we eventually abandon whatever it is that we were planning or working on ultimately failing.

    Dream killers are around you, you've met these people before and you even interact with them regularly. You might live with them, work next to them socialize with them. They're the kind of people who always seem to have an answer for everything. They're quick to give you advice and confident that they know what's best for everyone. They might even seem harmless in fact, it's sometimes comforting to trust in their perspective. Consciously or not their true nature is that they are dream killers. They are the people who will tell you that your aspirations are unrealistic, unsustainable, too risky, impossible, unreasonable, too imaginative, and even speak of them being ridiculous on and on. They will tell you that they're just trying to help out or offer guidance when they say these things. They won't admit that they're out to shoot down your dreams and have you fail. But you can't let these people shoot you down even if they are your family which could come as a surprise but it happens. Sometimes the worst dream killers can be found among those closest to us and since we don't choose the family we're born into, sometimes the people in our family circle don't always support our dreams. Family members might ridicule your dream or speak out of jealousy but simply identify such members of your family and avoid them or at least mentally tune them out.

Your friends can become dangerous dream killers too. Be very careful about who you share your dreams with, especially when your idea is in the early stages. Sometimes it's a good idea to ignore friendly advice and stick to your vision. The company you keep has a great impact on your life, social circles can boost your performance and help you get closer to your dream or kill them completely. Other dream killers can be found in the form of your colleagues and superior at work who have authority over you and might be crushing your dream as well. Your boss might feel threatened by your vision and actively prevent you from realizing your goals if that could translate into a promotion over him or you leaving the company for greener pastures. We cannot neglect our past for it can and does affect our future, failures teach us great life lessons. Instead of feeling ashamed of it, consider failure as a learning opportunity and a second change to do better. When you fail there is always an alternative door that opens. Embrace failure as part of your road to success and find strength in it to keep on chasing your dream. Stay fit and health because the way you feel physically drain you emotionally and intellectually. It's like trying to run with a stone in your shoes. You should never give up on your dreams despite how you feel because when your spirits are high and you have a purpose in life that could even be a motivation for you to recover quickly as its been proven scientifically that healing can partly be attributed to your thinking.

Dream killer are unfortunately unavoidable. No matter how hard you try, they're going to find you sooner or later because they are all around us. So it's important to know how to do deal with them. Know it's not really about you but rather their insecurities. Most dream killers have a reason for acting the way they do: most often it's to protect their way of life, being territorial like animals or fearing competition. They might feel or say they're trying to be helpful, and they may actually believe it, but what they're doing is actually about them. Parents can be dream killers and their fears can often reflect their way of thinking and they will act perhaps not with malicious intent but they can have a negative effect on your aspirations. Besides you parents other people may actually be afraid that you might actually make something great with your time and your life beyond what they have or could accomplish. That is why in a lot of cultures throughout the world before enterprising anything important in your life you don't reveal until it's a "Fait Accompli". Some people may not consciously try to pull you down, they're perhaps convinced that the safe and risk-free life is necessary, and your dreams threaten that ideology. They're so sure of it that your talk about wanting something else is deeply fear inducing. People often do not jump with joy when you launch a new project, they always expect something negative. When you succeed despite their negative attempts, you prove to them that you had the courage to go after your dreams and they did not have that same courage. Your success reveal many people's failures in life and people can get bitter in the face of such truth. Dream killers could be your family members, your parents, friends, colleagues or best friend who will try to stop you from taking action, because action defies their way of life and takes you to success. It's hard to often identify the dream killer because he comes disguised as a person close to us but you can't let just anyone and everyone mess with your aspirations.

You have the right to refuse people's opinions and do not take into consideration negative discouraging remarks. Many at times these people may not do it consciously so you should not take it personal that they do not share your enthusiasm, remember that it's not about you but rather their own insecurities, it's not really about your dreams or aspirations, or anything other than their inability to face their own fears. Turn to people that are receptive to your aspiration and will encourage you but most of all you need to arm yourself with a great dose of inspiration and a role model to follow preferably one that was in your same situation. Getting close to realizing your dream is a daunting task on its own because it's made harder by dream killers. The people around you who can potentially reduce your energy and enthusiasm, effectively preventing you from becoming everything you can be in life by discouraging you. One this we should take note of is that dream killers aren't only people and can be material or spiritual and factors such as we mentioned earlier; fear, cynicism, past failures, state of your health or fatigue. All of these take a great toll on your life and make it more difficult to reach your aspirations. In life you won't achieve anything until you find the courage to act on it despite discouragements. So much has been achieved in the word by people who faced great hardship but never backed down. If you can repeat to yourself daily that "you've got only one life to live" so that you can be motivated to act on your dreams and aspirations closer to your goals. Say to yourself that if you don't take this chance now, it's possible that you'll regret it later in your life. You should always go for it because you owe it to yourself to be or see how far you could go in life. Identifying a dream killer is key, knowing that they are all around us and can even be very close to us consciously not acting against our aspiration will provide us with better chances of success in life. We have to insure that we take out this negative factors from our lives so that we can face our destiny and reach our fullest potential, focus on achieving our dreams and aspirations. Action will be the key to success in anything in life also being aware and avoiding Dream Killers.

Get Rich Quick Build Wealth Now

Chapter V

How Money Works

How money works we all have a basic idea but how does it grow and relate to everything we do and aspire to be is what we need to master. Money buys things we know that and we have known that since the age of 3 when all we did was look for coin to go buy sweets. Money can make all your dreams come true; from getting anything you want in life to satisfying your needs and caring for the people you love. Get that money we won't emphasized that enough, throughout this book and we have made it clear that earning an income is absolutely critical not only to survive but also to build wealth. You need to be earning money to get rich. Thanks to Robert Kiyosaki's "Rich Dad Poor Dad" writings and such other books as "Cash Flow Quadrant," various methods of generating income are revealed to the public which was unaware of the existence or possibilities of different means of earning an income. These include holding a job, employment, self-employment, business ownership / management, passive income through profitable investing notably in real estate and the stock market.

Different methods produce a different perception of how to make money. This book has helped you understand and be aware of the various means in existence to earn money.

There is only one way to earn an income in this world, it's work and we would like someone to disprove this fact of course investment income is the result of work. Doing anything that produces income is work not that we encourage what is considered illegal but prostitution is work, drug dealing is work, stealing, house break in, scamming, fraud anything design to bring money your way requires action and is work. Ill gotten money does not last and comes with baggage and consequences that could see you lose it and whatever you could have built with it. No one should ever convince you to do anything illegal to earn money because that will set you back much more and cost you time in terms of prison time during which time you won't be able to build wealth.

In buying this book you have set yourself up to building wealth and getting rich which requires having the right attitude, information, planning and taking good decisions. There are time honored principles of building wealth; work to earn money, budget to save and stay out of debt; save to invest; build credit to control debt or avoid debt; and finally protect the wealth you have accumulated. Every rich person got his start somewhere and you will always hear stories of someone starting to earn money from the mail room until he worked his way up to the CEO position. You have entrepreneurs who started selling on the streets with very little capital to end up with a multinational corporation. A single mother who held two jobs and had a side business that became a success and made her a multi-millionaire.

As the old saying goes: "You have to have money to make money." So keeping yourself busy earning money is critical in building wealth no matter what your situation you need to find a way to make money, you have to change your mindset and believe that you can find a way to make more money. If you have a job, even though you might not like that job, give it everything that you've got, work as hard as you can as it could open up new opportunities for you. Good work never goes unnoticed, when working remember that it's a part of your plan to getting rich. Some people may start by working for someone as a way to keep earning an income but those that are able to directly venture into entrepreneurship all the better.

For obvious reasons being self-employed is like taking the highway to riches, entrepreneurship is not easy but it is a sure shot to getting rich faster than being employed. If you have the possibility to go from being employed to self-employed make the shift you will see you wealth building take a different turn and speed. To earn an income on your way to getting rich you must find yourself amongst one of these occupations: employee, the entrepreneur, the business owner, and the investor. The distinction made between the entrepreneur and the business owner is simply to size of the business as an entrepreneur will be an individual self-employed whereas a business owner will have a full business operation with staff and offering a service, or manufacturing a product.

As an employee to make more money you have to get to any of the other three occupations. Being in business will lead to a lot of failures before you adapt to a business that will finally pay off. Many businesses fail in their first 5 years of operations for several reasons but being persistent and diversifying the service offering will keep you active in business. The author created over 100 businesses that knew great success in the first year but then declined and failed within 5 years. In the end as a business owner your business will be the result of several business ventures that didn't work out, you may even lose money in some business ventures but you can't fear losing when trying to build a business.

This chapter's title is How Money Works, it may seem easier said than done but getting an income so as to have money is what we mean as an imperative for building wealth its elementary, but for those who are just starting out, or are in transition, this is the most fundamental step to getting rich. Once you are earning an income and have cut down on your expenses you should look into ways to increase your income. An article in Investopedia advises that there are two types of income earned and passive. Earned income comes from what you "do for a living," while passive income is derived from investments. The Investopedia, article published 27 of November 2017 titled "3 steps to building wealth" further states that: if you are lucky enough to be in the beginning of your career as in your early 20s and beginning your career or in the midst of a career change you can think about the following four considerations to decide how to derive your "earned income":

1. Consider what you enjoy. You will perform better and be more likely to succeed financially doing something you enjoy.
2. Consider what you're good at. Look at what you do well and how you can use those talents to earn a living.
3. Consider what will pay well. Look at careers using what you enjoy and do well that will meet your financial expectations.

4. Consider how to get there. Determine the education requirements, etc., needed to pursue your options.

Taking these considerations into account will put you on the right path. The key is to be open-minded and proactive. You should also evaluate your income situation annually. When earning an income and having investments, you'll be able to achieve your financial goals faster if you have financial goals and you make intentional financial decisions, setting goals, being intentional and taking action all play a crucial role in determining your success.

Building wealth is possible when you take action and take advantage of wealth-building tools and services that passively grow your money over time. This chapter simply asks you to get that money the best way you know how, work at it knowing that you getting rich depends on what you do to Get that Money.

We have heard time and again that "money rules the world" or that "money is the root of all evil" both of these adages can be very true in the sense that in a capitalistic society if you don't have money you have nothing and you are nothing even the things made by god meant to be free like friendship, love etc…… Financial Empowerment comes with so much and makes everything right and gets you closer to happiness. Financial empowerment is true freedom, morale and financial independence. So much comes with being financially empowered and that means achieving a wealth mentality. Often the result of long-term financial success depends on choices you make today and every day. So the earlier you start making financial decisions that help you build lasting financial independence the better. The earlier you start, the more time is on your side to build long-term wealth and attain financial empowerment.

It's important to master money and or be able to effectively manage that money. Today you will not hear people saying "money is the root of all evil" but rather lack of money is the root of all evil. Acquire knowledge on how to manage your money and build wealth, there are great wealth building tools available that work and can realistically make you financially wealthy. Let's look at how money works and how it should be managed by starting with understanding the meaning of assets, liabilities and net worth. We are working to get rich quick and build wealth now, which means we are looking to have NET WORTH.

ASSETS – LIABILITIES = NET WORTH

When creating wealth the more assets you have the better but there are many types of assets some that help you create more wealth and others that don't. The assets that help you increase your wealth by providing you with an income, return or increasing in value are:

- A business
- An interest baring savings account.
- Collectible artifacts.
- A retirement plan.
- Jewelry and precious metals.
- Stocks, bonds and mutual funds.
- A property.
- An intellectual property

Many assets we own in our daily lives like your cars, furnitures, household items, electronic items and clothes are assets because they have value, but they aren't wealth creating assets because they don't give you the possibility to earn money or rise in value like the others of course there are exceptions to the rule.

A liability is debt, money you owe and some liabilities can prevent you from building wealth, there is good debt and bad debt. Debt reduces net worth and the interest you pay on debt is money that cannot be saved or invested, it's an expense and it's just gone. Good debt will allow you for example to acquire a wealth building asset like a house or even a car used for business while a bad debt will simple allow you to consume. Bad debt carries interest to the principal amount your borrowed as well as other fees and that interest compounds, which is why the faster to pay off your debts the better. You have to keep track of your net worth and measure your wealth on your net worth. Having two million at the bank while owing two million does not make you rich.

When building your wealth your money will grow through compound interest helping as well and it will grow even faster because interest is paid on previously earned interest as well as on the original amount. We cannot talk about how money works or investment for that matter without mentioning the rule of 72. The Rule of 72 can help you estimate how your investment will grow over time. Simply divide the number 72 by your investment's expected rate of return to find out approximately how many years it will take for your investment to double in value. Example: Invest $10,000 today at a hypothetical 8 percent interest. Divide 72 by 8 and you get 9. This mean that your investment of 10,000 will double every nine years. In nine years, your 10,000 investment will be worth about 20,000, in 18 years about 40,000 and in 27 years, 80,000. The Rule of 72 also works if you want to find out the rate of return you need to make your money double. For example, if you have some money to invest and you want it to double in 10 years, what rate of return would you need? Divide 72 by 10 and you get 7.2. Your money will double in 10 years if your average rate of return is 7.2 percent.

When building wealth we have to understand the difference between saving and investing because the objective for both is often not the same and one performs better than the other. In building wealth you are seeking financial independent and at one point your money will be working harder than you and producing more money than you would or could when working. To reach financial independence you will have a strategy a plan to reach a certain amount that will then start generating more money than you can produce working so it's important to know the purpose of each tool at your disposal be it savings or investments. Let's look at the way both are defined.

Saving money is defined as placing earned income in cash in a zero risk environment, accessible at will, a variety of bank accounts; savings, notice deposits, call, checking, most money market invested in Treasury bill or government bond markets, savings will also include bonds and government treasury bills. All these tools available for saving money which is mostly a way to place or park your money before using it elsewhere should have your money ready and liquid at all times available on request. Saving money simply allows you to place your money somewhere while avoiding the effects of inflation.

To see the difference let's look at investing money, whose definition is placing your money in a situation that will allow for it to grow by generating income based on speculation that could see the value of your investment increase or reduce. Investment is putting your money at risk through product, business or transaction despite the fact that the placement is a calculated risk many external factors can influence the rate of return earned. Investment means buying an asset like real estate or stocks, bonds, a business with the intention that the investment will earn an income.

Based on the above definitions it's obvious what we need to do to increase or build wealth but the truth is that saving money will always be the first thing we do before engaging in business or investments so these two go hand in hand when building wealth. The growth of your money will now depend on the investment made that is why financial education or financial literacy is important when learning how to build wealth. Savings is placing your money in zero risk environment, earning interest at least to preserve the value by beating inflation while investing is taking a risk to even lose the value of your money to gain more money. When building wealth you will have to do both usually at the same time. To start investing you will need a certain amount of money which you may not have in the beginning and you will have to save as you earn. Once you have earned money which you placed into savings you can now invest.

Being ready to invest means you saved enough and now your money can start working for your and earn alongside you. You will be investing in not only earning a return on your investment, you will also be investing in a retirement fund, in acquisition of assets and protection of your assets. Protection of your assets will be critical as you build wealth, you need to protect your hard earned income from natural disasters, accidents and human interferences such as theft or vandalism. Tangible assets are part of your net worth and face many risks against which there are insurance products to protect. We have to remember that you are the first and most important factor in building wealth because everything will rely on you, your education and your actions; if you are unable to act you won't build wealth and like we said earlier tangible assets face many risks, you are your most precious asset when building wealth although you are not counted when the net worth is calculated. Staying fit and in good shape is critical, investing in health insurance is very important because of several reasons;

- Illness can come at any time and from anywhere be it an airborne flu epidemic or disease, you need to stay fit, to keep working and managing your wealth building plan.
- The cost of health care can set you back thousands and wipe out your savings and investments; so protecting yourself from the risk of falling sick or being involved in an accident is critical in building wealth.

When you work hard to earn money and build wealth it only makes sense to protect your health and wealth and various insurance companies will provide you with policies ranging from personal liability, to unemployment insurance, to health, to key person, to income, accidental damage, accidental liability and even in death you can protect your assets from creditors with credit life insurance, life insurance policies that cover all your debts and provide income to your family and children in case of premature death. It makes sense to protect what you have built through sweat blood and tears throughout your life. When using insurance to protect your assets here are a few tips:

• Group insurance provides savings in terms of premiums as you pay a lower premium than if you had it individually and this is typically available through your employer, professional associations or even social associations. Mutual insurance associations or companies typically offer lower premiums.

• You should always review you needs on a month to month basis or anytime there is a major change in your life, from child birth to change of employment, anticipate the needs of your family to be able to accurately decide on coverage and how much premium you can afford to pay.

• The higher the deductible which is the amount you pay first or the amount you are responsible for when making a claim, the lower your premium and that can help you save money.

Protecting your money also mean not being a mougou (fool), losing your hard earned money to a scam or a worthless product like buying a cheap electronic item you will have to buy again after 3 months.

How money works and knowing how to manage, spend, and invest your money will get you rich and change your life for the better. Financial literacy is not taught at school and these skills are often passed on from one generation to the other through our parents and usually time honored principals acquired by your family but rich families will have good wealth building habits that a poorer family will not have. We will look at these later in this book. The basic of knowing how to manage your money will remain the same for centuries to come. We all have very basic money management skills but when building wealth we are talking about gaining new skills that involve creating a budget, diversifying incomes streams and investing for the future. Management of money can seem tedious for many people as it involves accounting, one of the most boring jobs in the world. Dealing with a lot of numbers and calculations can cause a lot of stress if you can't make sense of the numbers. As we have demonstrated in previous chapters building wealth or managing money is about adopting a certain behavior towards money. Wealth building and how money works is about your state of mind, psychology, habits, and the set principles you apply to your daily life. For your money to work for you and improve your lifestyle to that of a rich person, you can't escape certain habits like spending less money than you earn in order to save money. Spending less than you earn will require budgeting and the discipline to stay within the budget. Only a budget can help you make out how much you are saving from your earnings. Those who do well save at least 30% of their income.

Setting goals for the money you are saving is very critical and one of the good habits to have. You money must have a purpose or it will be lost. The purpose of saving money can be from future investment, launching of a business or an emergency fund for unpredictable events. Your money must also make money so part of your plans when saving should include making your money work just as hard as you work. When your money can generate and exceed what you can earn you will understand why the rich keeps getting richer. The fundamental of how money works will never change and for the next 100 years will remain the same just as our ancestors did it before us. Perhaps new products will come in the market in the form of investments but the principles will be the same. More sophisticated money management tools may become available allowing you to better invest or manage your money, investing principals will not change. It's neither safe nor advisable to keep a large amount of cash under your mattress, it could burn or be stolen amongst the risks it's exposed to. As stated previously the use of a savings account to park our money while waiting for the right amount or investment tool to put the money in is where money should be in the short terms. Banks can hold your money and allow you to access it anytime you need to be it at the branch or through bank cards. Setting up a savings bank account is easy and most banks want you to open an account with them and would offer you good rates or other gift to do so. We live in the internet age and technology makes a lot of things possible to a point where you can even open your bank account online without ever going into a branch. There are even virtual banks or ebanks that are branchless, everything is done electronically, online. There are so many choices for you in opening up a savings bank account, typically online ebanks have lower fees because of lower overheads but depending on your needs find an banking institution that will satisfy your needs in terms of service and banking fees. Online electronic banks typically offer lower banking fees and better interest rates on your money that way your money earns a little extra money just for keeping it in your account compared with traditional banks which have higher operating costs associated with physical branches.

When saving your money with a bank are you curious to know how it works? Where it goes? Well the bank basically uses bank deposits to invest, they provide your money to someone in need against interest or they purchase assets that generate income such as treasury bills some types of bonds and they provide short term credit facilities against interest. What the bank does with your money is basically the same you will be doing with your money when investing. You will not be providing credit facilities but making investments or making your money available when and where needed to generate money. To save money you have to budget and it just means knowing where your money is going and planning ahead how you spend it. You may not necessarily want to seat and determine where each and every dollar is spent therefore a summarized budget with main title expenses will be ideal for you.

When building wealth debt is the enemy and credit cards tend to promote consumer credit the worst kind of credit anyone could have when trying to build wealth. In our society we can no longer live without credit and building a credit history is important and will allow us to acquire good income producing assets or value increasing assets. Income producing and value increasing assets are the biggest contributors to wealth building and financial independence those typically start in the form of debt for most people. A mortgage on a home or building is a good debt in the sense that the asset will grow faster than the interest to be paid on it. Credit cards are using in the beginning part of building up credit so as to access larger amount of money in credit. So building up your credit and protecting your credit worthiness is very important. Start building credit with your credit cards because fresh out of school you won't get a car if you do not have a credit history and you won't be able to buy a house if you don't have a credit rating or have a bad credit rating. Nowadays it's easy to get a credit card because there is a lot of competition but just as easy you can get a credit card it's very hard to get out of debt. The credit card kind of debt can put you in a hole that's hard to climb out of for many years if you do not carefully spend or budget. But credit cards can also be really useful when properly used; simply don't use a credit card to buy things you can't afford or don't absolutely need. Instead, only buy something if you have the money in your account right now, and pay off your card's balance every month to avoid a situation of compounding negative interest. Use the credit card only when you have the money to pay for whatever you want to purchase as online store typically only take credit cards.

The credit card trap is very easy to fall into, here is how it works; banks for the most part issue credit cards to people but there are credit card companies that only issue credit cards and small loans through the cards as principal credit. You are charged interest on the principal credit which is an amount that is made available to you when you buy anything using the credit card. Once you have spent using the credit card the credit card issuer starts charging you interest calculated on a monthly basis based on an annual rate. You are typically required to pay back part of the principal credit along with interest but if you don't pay back the amount you owe will grow and the interest you were to pay will also grow at a set percentage making it more expensive to repay. If you don't pay on time you end up paying interest on ineptest you were to pay for the principal amount your borrowed to buy whatever you bought with the credit card. When using the credit card and paying you need to insure that you not only pay the principal amount but also the interest and even a little more if you can. The interest charged on your account is typically indicated as an annual percentage rate (or APR), but it's calculated on a daily basis and billed monthly. Each month, the credit card issuer will charge you the previous month's interest on the balance you owe and if you did not pay the previous month that means the principal amount plus the interest that was payable. The objective of a credit card is to keep you indebted and the banks usually collect the interest on the minimum payment they require you to pay which means you will basically pay them for life or at least 10 years depending on what percentage of the principal they apply to the minimum payment if you don't pay something extra. If you only pay the minimum amount due as they ask monthly, most of your payment will go towards interest meaning your balance will remain high, and keep generating interest for you to pay monthly. Always pay more than the minimum amount indicated as payment by the banks on your credit cards to get out of the debt spiral.

We said earlier that credit cards are bad debts and the source of a lot of depression when misused so now let's take a look at the advantages of using a credit card.

If you are robbed and your wallet is stolen or lost and all the money in it is used, you are almost guaranteed it's a loss even if the thief is caught, he goes to jail and your money is gone. But on the other hand credit cards are considered as cash with the difference that if you are robbed or lose the cards and money is used if you report the incident within a certain amount of time you will receive 100% refund of you money.

Whatever you buy using the credit card is also guaranteed, many credit cards issuers insure that merchants selling to card holders offer better warranties, protection against damages, loss, etc.… buying on credit card provides you with better quality products and services in the end. Your credit card typically has a lot of benefits you may not even be aware of but are part of your contract.

Some credit cards will offer you rewards when spending these rewards will range from cash to free gifts and should you manage your pending carefully which is the objective of the rewards, making you spend but if you mange spending carefully you will rip the rewards as a bonus for using the card.

Another advantage of your credit cards is that it's useful for creating and improving your credit score kept by the credit bureau whenever you have and use credit facilities anywhere. Banks and credit card companies want to insure that whenever someone gets credit they will pay back and as a result credit checks are typical whenever you apply for credit and your credit score will determine if and how much you credit you will be accorded. So as you use credit facilities a credit scoring systems keeps track of your repayment history, this is essentially a report that details your history of borrowing money and estimates how likely you are to pay money back. Financial institutions use this score to determine how much you can borrow, how much you'll be charged in interest, and how many lines of credit (like credit cards, car loans, or mortgages) you can have open. Building a good credit history is important whenever you plan on acquiring large assets like a home. The better your credit score, the better credit cards you'll be able to get, and the better loans, lower interest you'll be able to get for a house, car or any other asset you want to acquire. Your credit score also determined if you will be allowed access to certain services such as utilities and whether they will require you to put up a security deposit or not.

Credit scoring as become very important for access to certain services as most companies when to be able to plan and budget on their incomes and don't want to deal with dab debtors or loses that they would have to write off. There are several credit reporting agencies charged with keeping track of your borrowing and credit repayment and they will grade you on a variety of factors. These agencies typically look at a number of areas to grade you: Your repayment history; they check if you are paying your credit on time and usually this forms part of the most important criteria in scoring you. Your debt to credit ratio; the closer you are to your credit limit the worst, if you are granted credit and you use more than 50% of it your score will be worse than if you only use 30% of your granted credit. Put simply, this is how much money you're currently borrowing across all of your accounts, versus how much you're allowed to borrow in total. This is the second biggest factor in determining your credit score. Length of credit history; the longer you have lines of credit open, the better for your score. Types of credit; the mix of credit accounts you have can also benefit your score. Credit cards are considered higher risk than other forms of credit you could receive. Credit checks; Every time you try to open a new line of credit, that request is logged with the reporting agency. More credit checks usually means more of a risk (because they assume you're either borrowing too much or have been turned down too many times).

When using credit if you handle your finances well, you usually shouldn't have to do much to manage your credit score, pay at least the minimum on time every month keeping in mind that paying the minimum may not be good for you in the long run. You can typically repair your credit and there are many voluntary agencies out there that can assist you rebuild your credit. Even in case of bankruptcy you can rebuild your credit although you may have to wait a number of years for some bad marks to be removed from your credit report.

When finally in control of your money knowing how it works, budgeting and spending carefully you will be comfortable able to move to investments, the earlier you start saving, the more money you'll have later to invest. Money matters are very serious matters we cannot neglect as if we fail we stand to suffer in our old age and condemn our children to poverty or a life of struggles.

When you have saved some money investing it doesn't have to be complicated you will have access to financial advisors who can help you make choices based on your financial objectives. Getting started with long-term investments will often be one of the hardest parts of your financial life because, when you're just starting out, you don't have much money and you have many needs. Investing is an overwhelming area of finance, so start small and learn what you can do to grow your money requires a good plan and support from financial planner and advisors who know How Money Works.

An investment in knowledge always pays the best interest.
Benjamin Franklin

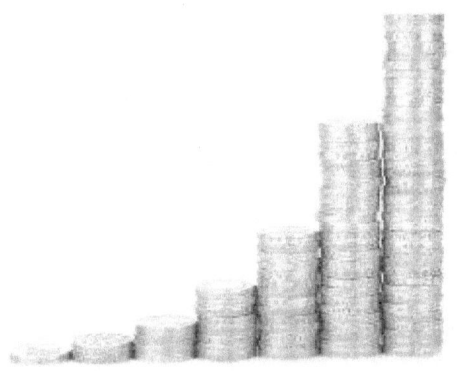

Get Rich Quick Build Wealth Now

Chapter VI

Psychological Conditioning

Psychological conditioning is plain simply the wealth mentality we have talked about throughout this book. It's getting into the state of mind needed to set yourself up to achieve your aspirations in our case Get Rich Quick, Build Wealth Now. If you believe that money is the root of all evil, your aspirations to gaining riches will certainly fail. Negative thoughts about money or wealth will work against you therefore conditioning yourself and your behavior towards money will instead work for you in your ambition to build wealth. Psychological conditioning is what we are taught to value, which might not be authentic to our own character. This is true for external things like television, fashion and trends in general, but it's even truer for our behavior.

Humans are suggestive beings, we may be see ourselves emulating other people having been psychologically conditioned. We are psychologically conditioned by the work we do, parents, religion, school and our society in general. If it was not for government stopping marketing companies from inserting subliminal messages in songs and commercials, marketing executives would have had all of us now hooked into some kind of product, unconsciously. We are taught, from a young age, who we are and how to be and think. Rather than being encouraged to find these things out for ourselves, we're taught to listen to what we're told, regardless if it's true for us. Psychological conditioning that is making us bypass our own personal development and growth through as an example: external marketing and messages that impact our minds. We should be aware that our conditioned behavior and systems come from messages penetrating our minds through social media, marketing and the news. We may be unconsciously conditioned but in the end the choice is ours. The awareness of the fact that our environment can shape us and how we perceive things should give us the opportunity to place ourselves in better situations. We should not be in around too many negative things.

Think positive when it comes to money and understand it as a problem solver. As previously mentioned the only difference between you and rich people, is your mindset. You can empower your brain to think logically, faster, positive and become more focused through various psychological conditioning programs or systems available almost everywhere now, even free of charge on the World Wide Web. We have mentioned neuro linguistic programming as an option, simply turn on the recording and you will be well on your way to influencing your beliefs, enabling you to achieve any goal you put your mind to with ease. You will be literally able to program your brain for financial abundance and success in general. Katherine Hurst who is a leading motivational speaker on the Laws of Attraction advises on audio programs designed to empower your brain so as to 'program' your brain for success and get a rich person's mentality. Chapter I also looked at Neuro linguistic programming a method of influencing brain behavior through the use of language and other types of communication to enable a person to "recode" the way the brain responds to stimuli and manifest new and better behaviors. We will not repeat in detail Neuro-Linguistic Programming as we have done above but simply highlight its use which often incorporates hypnosis and self-hypnosis to help achieve the change wanted. NLP Applications in everyday life include; Change work – Education – Training - Sales – Leadership – Marketing – Therapy

It is true that our environment has a lot to do with our way of life, be it the people around us, our thinking and the self-imposed limitations we may have. For those people who think they are simply surrounded by negative energy and environment, perhaps neuro-linguistic programming might be the solution. Getting rich quick by any means necessary means employing any tried tested solution available to equip you to get rich.

Neuro-linguistic programming is a method of influencing brain behavior through the use of language and other types of communication to enable a person to "recode" the way the brain responds to stimuli and manifest new and better behaviors. Neuro-Linguistic Programming often incorporates hypnosis and self-hypnosis to help achieve the change that is wanted. Neuro Linguistic Programming began its life early in the 1970s when an Associate Professor from the University of California, Santa Cruz, USA, John Grinder, teamed up with an undergraduate Richard Bandler who invented the term "Neuro-Linguistic Programming" and defined it as: "a model of interpersonal communication chiefly concerned with the relationship between successful patterns of behavior and the subjective experiences (esp. patterns of thought) underlying them" and "a system of alternative therapy based on this which seeks to educate people in self-awareness and effective communication, and to change their patterns of mental and emotional behavior."

Don't panic we have kept this book's language simple so it's easy to understand and we will continue that way, Neuro-linguistic Programming (NLP) today is mostly used for personal development and for financial success in business in particular and life in general.

This NLP method of improving life can be broken down as follows:

Neuro; each individual has established their own unique mental filtering system for processing the millions of bits of data being absorbed through the senses. Our first mental map of the world is constituted of internal images, sounds, tactile awareness, internal sensations, tastes and smells that form as result of the neurological filtering process.

Linguistic; we then assign personal meaning to the information being received from the world outside. Language to the internal images is assigned, sounds and feelings, tastes and smells, thus forming everyday conscious awareness.

Programming; the behavioral response that occurs as a result of neurological filtering processes and the subsequent linguistic map.

Neuro Linguistic Programming began with John Grinder who teamed up with Richard Bandler. Both men had a fascination with human excellence which charted a path for them to model behavioral patterns of selected geniuses. They modelled three people, Fritz Perls, Virginia Satir and Milton Erickson, these geniuses were outstanding as professional agents of change, working in the domain of therapy. All three geniuses, Perls, Satir and Erickson performed their magic from a perspective of unconscious excellence. The geniuses did not present Grinder and Bandler with a conscious description of their behavior. The modelers (Grinder and Bandler) unconsciously absorbed the patterning inherent in the geniuses and then provided a description. With little direct knowledge of each of the geniuses specialty and little knowledge of the field of psychotherapy as a whole, Grinder and Bandler over a two year period set out with enthusiasm bordering on fervor, to explicate selected portions of the geniuses' behavior. They coded the results of their work in language-based models using the patterns of transformational grammar as the descriptive vocabulary. Through NLP Modelling Grinder and Bandler made explicit the tacit skills of the geniuses and NLP was born.

In 1975 Grinder and Bandler presented the first two NLP models to the world in the volumes "Structure of Magic I and II." The volumes published by the respected publishing house "Science and Behavior Books inc" put NLP on the map and interest in the new field of NLP spread quickly. People in fields related to communication, behavior and change sought to learn how they too could get amazing results when doing change work. Grinder and Bandler willingly offered training courses in the application of their models. The training courses Bandler and Grinder conducted - proved that the NLP models were transferable to others, meaning the learners could use the NLP models successfully in their own work.

NLP Applications in everyday life include; *Change work – Education – Training - Sales – Leadership – Marketing - Therapy*

NLP has now grown into an international field and people excelling as a result of applying Neuro Linguistic Programming in their professions and personal lives.

There are so many suggestions on how to get rich and there is a lot of information in the public domain that is available to anyone seeking to improve their lives. Getting rich is a matter of choices, behaviors and mentality, limitations exist but adaptations to specific situations can level the playing field for everyone and achieving riches whether you have education or are illiterate, handicapped or abled bodied you can make it to financial independence. The system we live in is not designed to make people rich in fact only a few people get the wealth and the rest of the people must work to keep the few people rich but there are ways to get out of this system and join the rich. This has been going on for millenniums and unfortunately the average person has internalized this system and for you to get out of the system requires a lot of work as we have illustrated above.

It's important to psychologically condition yourself and get away from a poor man's mentality which does not attract wealth but keep you in perpetual poverty. There are differences between rich people and poor people in the way they behave:

A poor person will always be very skeptical and ambivalent while a rich person will be more trusting and decisive. Rich people more so that poor people reportedly leave there car and house doors opened. Trust will always allow one to have an open minded to be exposed to opportunities whereas the converse will shut down access to opportunities.

People who are poor are always looking for the problems instead of the solutions. They end up blaming their environment, circumstances, jobs, weather, government, and will make an extensive list of excuses as to why they cannot be successful. Whereas rich people understand that everything happens for a reason. Rather than letting life happen to them, they take direct action and make big things happen. They put aside all the excuses and eradicate their blame lists because they have to do what must be done.

Poor people often make assumptions instead of checking the facts or asking questions to get the truth, they never make a true attempt when it comes to getting what they want. Rich people ask the questions to know the truth, they believe if you begin to ask questions, you will save yourself a lot of hassle. The power is in the hands of those who ask the right questions. They don't answer your questions, question your answers.

The poor does not take ownership and responsibility for a lot of things and they have a tendency of thinking in terms of I whereas the rich will think in terms of WE.

The poor when shopping will always look for the cheapest overlooking the quality and the reason the item is cheap. The poor forgets that the cheapest is sometimes the most expensive in that the cheap item will not last and may have to be purchased again after a few months. A quality item costing more will last longer and save the buyer from having to buy another one again. Rich people want the best, they look for quality. They don't limit themselves to price and often seek service while they shop.

Time is money but not for the poor person, because for the poor money is more valuable, while time is invaluable as something you can never get back when money lost or stolen you can get again but time you never get that back. The majority of people trade time for money and never realize their true potential because of it. Rich people that time is more important than money and never trade time for money.

When a poor person sees an opportunity, they find out how others are doing it and emulates them. Most often, they never consider another way of doing it. Instead, they settle in the belief that doing what others are doing is the best thing they can do for themselves. Rich people create and blaze new trails.

Poor people complain, condemn, and criticize. Most poor people have learned how to be poor from their predecessors. Their family members have conditioned them to believe that everything is "wrong" instead of right. Rich people praise and enjoy their blessings. Rich people know that they have many privileges and they don't take it for granted. Because of their appreciation of gifts, love, and circumstances, they are able to generate more. Many times, what gets praised gets prospered.

Poor people seek amateur advice. They often listen to the opinions of others and seek approval from acquaintances. They believe almost everything they hear without questioning authority. They accept opinions as facts and prohibit themselves from doing research once satisfied with an answer. Rich people on the other hand seek expert advice. Those who are rich have learned to think for themselves. If they cannot figure out something, they seek expert advice. Usually, they pay for the advice and are given a wide variety of options. They learn the experts only make suggestions, which means that they aren't particularly confined to a specific action.

Poor people will have that big screen flat television, poor people take a lot of time to drift off to sporadic images of which they often have little to no control over. They use their free time to avoid the art of thinking (which is the most challenging task) and zone out to what many have conformed to believe is "entertainment." Rich people have big libraries, they educate themselves and read a lot of books. They use their knowledge in a way that benefits them. Instead of drifting off in random activities, they seek to get within their minds to understand themselves, others, and the world in which they live. In fact, as your personal library increase over the years, so will your home. I can attest to this!

Wealth really does change everything and those of high social class do tend to see themselves **much differently** than others. Wealth (and the pursuit of it) has been linked with **immoral behavior**. Psychologists who study the impact of wealth and inequality on human behavior have found that money can powerfully influence our thoughts and actions in ways that we're often not aware of, no matter our economic circumstances. Although wealth is certainly subjective, most of the current research measures wealth on scales of income, job status or measures of socioeconomic circumstances, like educational attainment and intergenerational wealth.

Here are seven things you should know about the psychology of money and wealth. More money, less empathy? Several studies have shown that wealth may be at odds with empathy and compassion. Research published in the journal *Psychological Science* also found that people of lower economic status were better at reading others' facial expressions an important marker of empathy than wealthier people.

"A lot of what we see is a baseline orientation for the lower class to be more empathetic and the upper class to be less [so]," study co-author Michael Kraus told TIME. "Lower-class environments are much different from upper-class environments. Lower-class individuals have to respond chronically to a number of vulnerabilities and social threats. You really need to depend on others so they will tell you if a social threat or opportunity is coming and that makes you more perceptive of emotions."

While a lack of resources fosters *greater* emotional intelligence, having more resources can cause bad behavior in its own right. University of Berkeley research found that even *fake* money could make people behave with less regard for others. Researchers observed that when two students played monopoly, one having been given a great deal more Monopoly money than the other, the wealthier player expressed initial discomfort, but then went on to act aggressively, taking up more space and moving his pieces more loudly, and even taunts the player with less money.

Wealth can cloud moral judgment.

It is no surprise in this world to learn that wealth may cause a sense of moral entitlement. A **UC Berkeley study** found that in San Francisco where the law requires that cars stop at crosswalks for pedestrians to pass **drivers of luxury cars** were four times less likely than those in less expensive vehicles to stop and allow pedestrians the right of way. They were also more likely to cut off other drivers.

Another study suggested that merely thinking about money could lead to unethical behavior. **Researchers from Harvard and the University of Utah** found that study participants were more likely to lie or behave immorally after being exposed to money related words.

"Even if we are well intentioned, even if we think we know right from wrong, there may be factors influencing our decisions and behaviors that we're not aware of," University of Utah associate management professor Kristin Smith-Crowe, one of the study's co-authors, **told Market Watch.**

Wealth has been linked with addiction.

While money itself doesn't cause addiction or substance abuse, wealth has been linked with a higher susceptibility to addiction problems. A number of studies have found that affluent children are more vulnerable to substance abuse issues, potentially because of high pressure to achieve and isolation from parents. Studies also found that kids who come from wealthy parents aren't necessary exempt from adjustment problems in fact, research found that on several measures of maladjustment, high school studies of high socioeconomic status received higher scores than inner-city students. Researchers found that these children may be more likely to internalize problems, which has been linked with substance abuse.

But it's not just adolescents: Even in adulthood, the rich outdrink the poor by more than 27 percent.

Money itself can become addictive.

The pursuit of wealth itself can also become a compulsive behavior. As Psychologist Dr. Tian Dayton explained, a compulsive need to acquire money is often considered part of a class of behaviors known as process addictions, or "behavioral addictions," which are distinct from substance abuse:

These days, the idea of process addictions is widely accepted. Process addictions are addictions that involve a compulsive and/or an out of control relationship with certain behaviors such as gambling, sex, eating and yes, even money... There is a change in brain chemistry with a process addiction that's similar to the mood altering effects of alcohol or drugs. With process addictions engaging in a certain activity, say viewing pornography, compulsive eating or an obsessive relationship with money, can kick start the release of brain/body chemicals, like dopamine, that actually produce a "high" that's similar to the chemical high of a drug. The person who is addicted to some form of behavior has learned, albeit unconsciously, to manipulate his own brain chemistry.

While a process addiction is not a chemical addiction, it does involve **compulsive behavior** in this case, an addiction to the good feeling that comes from receiving money or possessions which can ultimately lead to negative consequences and harm the individual's well-being. Addiction to spending money sometimes known as **shopaholism** is another, more common type of money-associated process addiction.

Wealthy children may be more troubled.

Children growing up in wealthy families may seem to have it all, but having it all may come at a high cost. Wealthier children tend to be more distressed than lower-income kids, and are at high risk for anxiety, depression, substance abuse, eating disorders, cheating and stealing. Research has also found high instances of binge-drinking and marijuana use among the children of high-income, two-parent, white families.

"In upwardly mobile communities, children are often pressed to excel at multiple academic and extracurricular pursuits to maximize their long-term academic prospects a phenomenon that may well engender high stress, "psychologist Suniya Luthar in "The Culture Of Affluence." "At an emotional level, similarly, isolation may often derive from the erosion of family time together because of the demands of affluent parents' career obligations and the children's many after-school activities."

We tend to perceive the wealthy as "evil."

On the other side of the spectrum, lower-income individuals are likely to judge and stereotype those who are wealthier than themselves, often judging the wealthy as being "cold." (Though it is also true that the poor struggle with their own set of societal stereotypes.)

Rich people tend to be a source of envy and distrust, so much so that we may even take pleasure in their struggles, according to Scientific American. University of Pennsylvania research demonstrated that most people tend to link perceived profits with perceived social harm. When participants were asked to assess various companies and industries (some real, some hypothetical), both liberals and conservatives ranked institutions perceived to have higher profits with greater evil and wrong-doing across the board, independent of the company or industry's actions in reality.

Money can't buy happiness (or love).

We tend to seek money and power in our pursuit of success (and who doesn't want to be successful, after all?), but it may be getting in the way of the things that really matter: Happiness and love. There is no direct correlation between income and happiness. After a certain level of income that can take care of basic needs and relieve strain (some say $50,000 a year, some say $75,000), wealth makes hardly any difference to overall well-being and happiness and, if anything, only harms well-being: Extremely affluent people actually suffer from higher rates of depression.

Some data has suggested money itself doesn't lead to dissatisfaction instead, it's the ceaseless striving for **wealth and material possessions** that may lead to unhappiness. Materialistic values have even been linked with **lower relationship satisfaction.** But here's something to be happy about: More Americans are beginning to look beyond money and status when it comes to defining success in life. Only around one-quarter of Americans still believe that wealth determines success, **according to a 2013 Life Twist study.**

Your mentality counts for a lot and changing it from established bad habits will not be easy so psychological conditioning is imperative. To get a true perspective on how to become rich, you must study rich people. After all, you become what you study. If you're currently surrounded by people who aren't yet rich, just do the opposite of what they do. Soon enough, you'll be able to reach your financial dreams!

Conditioning yourself to build wealth will require a shift in mentality and once you are wealthy, to stay wealthy and manage being wealthy will also take great efforts as we have seen that with wealth could come some side effects. Despite the problems that come with being wealthy, we suggest that being wealthy is better than being poor. This chapter will now reveal what most readers probably would have never read or heard before, pertaining to money, getting rich, building wealth and the psychological conditioning required. We have come to understand that the god particle which links everything that exists in this universe can be harmonized or controlled by our brain. You have certainly heard that we human being only use about 10% of the capacity of our brain. Imagine if we could reach 50% capacity and what we could do. For the most part the major use of our brain is limited to what we do unconsciously from breathing, smelling to organ functions to healing when wounded etc..... the brain is responsible for all these which do not depend on our conscious thinking, whether we want or are conscious of it or not when we are wounded, the wound will heal, same for breathing and many other functions we do not consciously control. In this chapter we are talking about psychological conditioning which means affecting the way we receive perceive and treat information we are exposed to.

We need to understand that we are made of the same stuff money is made of in fact anything that exits is made of the same god particle as long as its matter the god particle is also known as the Higgs boson. All matters that exist are made of the same subatomic particles; humans, things and animals. When you break everything down to the tiniest of any matter in existence you see that we are all made of the Higgs boson. The Higgs Boson are different subatomic particles which are responsible for giving matter different properties particularly mass. Particles, like protons and neutrons, have mass as do almost everything in existence; man, animals, plants, objects and money. Others, like photons, do not have mass. The Higgs boson, or "God particle," is believed to be the particle which gives mass to matter therefore man and money are made of the same stuff. Every object in existence is made up of matter, anything you can touch physically. The more matter an object has, the bigger it is, and the more mass it has. Mass is measured in kilograms, kg, or grams, g. Things that have a big mass are harder to move, or harder to stop when in motion than objects with little mass. Let's sum it up; Atoms, electrons, neutrons and protons are the basic building blocks of matter and matter is made of mass, it's palpable. Neutrons and protons make up the nucleus of an atom, while electrons circle this nucleus. The number of these particles that make up an atom are what help differentiate elements from one another. An atom is comprised of a nucleus containing neutrons and protons, as well as electrons that orbit the nucleus. This particle is the tiniest object that can retain the properties of an element. It cannot be broken up or divided by any chemical methods. An electron is bound to and orbits the nucleus of an atom. This indivisible particle has a negative charge. Its mass is 1/1,837 of the mass of a proton. Located in the nucleus of atoms, neutrons have mass slightly lower than those of protons. This indivisible particle gets its name for the fact that it has no electrical charge. It is 1,839 times the size in mass of an electron. Proton; Elements get their atomic number based on the number of protons found in each atom. This indivisible particle in the nucleus of an atom carries a positive charge. A proton has a mass 1,837 times greater than that of an electron. We have gone through all the trouble of explaining how mass relates to matter and what matter is made of so you can understand that atoms are energy. Einstein submitted that mass and energy are one in the same. Factually, mass can convert into energy and vice-versa. All matter in existence that you can see and touch is a manifestation of energy. In conclusion since humans are matter and energy and considering the fact that money is matter hence it is also energy. Thus we see that matter itself is energy. However in chemical reactions, it may use its own internal energy, or absorb energy from surroundings in the form of heat, light etc.

Now that we know money is energy and that energy makes things work as it is defined in most dictionaries, we want to further suggest that in popular belief energies can attract each other. Our mind body and soul are composed of energy and our feelings translate into different vibrations. The people with the same vibes will tend to be together meaning positive people will hang with positive people while the negative people, complainers, drama kings and queens, haters will tend to like each other's company. In recent years there has been new developments in the field of psychology and the development of the Laws of Attraction. The Laws of attraction looks at everything being made of energy and like energy being able to attract like energy. A positive mental attitude towards anything will place you in tune with that subject and possibly attracted to it. These laws of attractions work for everything in your life be it to attract friends, decision in your favor, relationships and even money can be attracted. The Law of attraction is based on the fact that like energy attract like energy based on the law of vibration which states that we attract what we are sending out so positive energies attract positive energies and vice versa for negative energies. So working on raising your positive energy towards people, events in your life and money is key to successfully getting your way. You can basically wish your way into anything, healing faith comes to mind. Across the world millions of people through faith and the positive believe that God can cure them often walk away satisfied that they have been cured. Science has explained this as a placebo effect, meaning with or without medication people have been cured because of the simple belief that they have been administered a cure. Scientific experiments went as far as faking surgery and letting a patient believe they had gone through surgery and to the amazement of doctors the patient showed signs of relief.

We are presenting really very serious stuff that should have you be a lot more illuminated than the average person that did not read this book. Humans actually have powers to influence their environment, powers through the mastery of positive energy and the brain. The world as we know it has a specific energy flow which manages all aspects of our lives; from our likes to money. Have you ever noticed that whenever you dread something that is exactly when it happens? Or at least the chances of it happening are much higher than when you firmly believe it will not happen. \The United States of America is the greatest nation on earth not because it really is but because the vast majority of Americans think that way despite never having travelled outside the United States. They may not be aware that there are countries where there are better laws and freedoms, better social services and an economic system that is fairer to the population allowing more people to make more money and having a lower income disparity. It's easier to build wealth in certain countries as opposed to others because of varying factors such as infrastructures and people's mentality in general. Throughout Africa people are scared to part ways with their money and very hardly let go unless absolutely necessary. You then have long drawn-out negotiations to close a sale, and the banking system reflects the same mentality; that is why African banking institutions are the most liquid in the world. In Africa people will not easily live on credit or borrow as compared to the western countries of Europe and America, whose consumer debts are many times those of Africans. So building wealth in Africa will vary slightly for entrepreneurs and business owners who may not be able to expand their businesses rapidly as others would in Europe and American due to the presence not only of financial institutions but also angel investors or venture capitalist funds. Despite these differences the laws of attraction remain the same and attracting money or wealth to you is possible.

We have the ability to redirect the energies around us, money and wealth being energies we can attract it to us. Creating an environment that will allow you to earn money and keep it mean, creating energies that people will want to have or be associated with in exchange for money. You have to have something to offer some kind of service or knowledge and offer it in a creative, exciting and positive way. To break ranks with the system that perpetually keeps you in poverty or struggle for money and be what you want to be in life you need to break away from what the world says you are or should be. To realize our fullest potential in life we have to blaze our own trail, create the person we want to be, a character that suits you and allows you to be positive, create a power around you with positive energies, optimism will allow you to get more out of life. We have to remember that wealth will move or part of wealth will move from someone else's possession to yours and for that to happen they have to willfully accept the transfer. A person having dinner in a restaurant that is served by a smiling waitress or waiter will have a better experience that is the waiter or waitress is not smiling and the person may not again come to the establishment. Positive vibes attract positive vibes, limiting yourself from having negative thoughts, gossiping our people and being jealous of people will work against you instead we need to be positive and be happy for anyone that is successful.

Our brain has a lot to do with our success as it is the key and master of our destiny. Properly channeling our brain into a wealth building mindset to succeed is critical as there are too many factors out there working against us. The political and economic systems in place are meant to keep people down and wanting more and more money so that money generated will maintain the system. Poverty is out to get everyone and no matter how smart and how hard you work the pitfalls are many and you need to prepare for it therefore the importance of Psychological conditioning.

Get Rich Quick Build Wealth Now

Chapter VII

Principles of Building Wealth

Principles of building wealth will vary from one person to another in fact two people will be saying the same things but perhaps using different words and context. Bill Gates once said, "It's not your fault if you were born poor, but it's your fault if you die poor." Bill Gates is obviously of these who believe being rich is much better than being poor. We have learned so much throughout the various chapters of this book and we have made a list of suggestions as what we should consider as principles of building wealth. These principles have not changed for a thousand years and remain applicable, so many people keep looking left and right looking for the secrets to getting rich. Usually when so many people look for a secret for so long it means there is no secret, today the required knowledge is available in the public domain. Getting rich and building wealth today is a matter of will and action.

There are time honored principles of building wealth;
- Your wealth building journey starts with you getting to work producing and generating income by any means necessary but

legally; work to earn money, create various revenues streams. There is no wealth building or becoming rich without an income, money will not fall from the sky and waiting on a rich uncle to die to inherit wealth is not recommended if you did not develop a wealth mentality before getting that money.

- Once you have created various sources of income with money coming in to you, you must control your spending and not let your wants dominate your needs; budget to save. We spend money on unnecessary things we want and not what we need so budgeting is very critical and having the discipline to respect the budget is what will lead to savings.

- Successful restraint and budgeting will allow us to see more of our money and realize savings. With money saved you can take advantage of various vehicles that will grow our money faster by investing in the stock market or in businesses; save to invest. Saving money means parking our unused money in safe keeping instruments like saving accounts with the aim of preserving the value of the money against inflation. But the aim is to move the money from savings to investments.

- You can't save if you are in debt and you can't build wealth if you have huge liabilities, the more money you have saved and invested will allow you to have credit balances as opposed to debt which carry interest; build credit to control debt or avoid debt. Your journey to building wealth will require that you become debt free, it's only once you have eliminated debt that you can see your net worth. Once you have saved money you will have to invest it to grow your wealth. Only investments will allow you to grow your wealth; there are several investment instruments available from the stock market, to the bond and real estate. Acquisition of hard income producing assets will be key. Assets that appreciate in value while producing incomes.

- And finally protect the wealth you have accumulated, the hard assets and properties are part of your net worth which determines your level of wealth but if something happens to the property like fire or else you lose what you would have worked hard for years, so it makes sense to protect your investments with insurance products which offer the best hedge against loses of wealth. In protecting your net worth you will not just be looking out for fires, you will have to insure your life, returns, beat the inflation rates as well and keep a budget.

The above sums up essentially what is into the principles of wealth building. We further provide these long held beliefs to help inspire you:

Pay yourself first, as opposed to spending your hard earned money on paying everybody else, have a payment made to yourself as a percentage of the money you made. That money can be saved or invested and even placed for retirement but it's supposed to be stacked before you pay all your bills. If you manage to put away anywhere from 10 to 30% of your income before spending anything you will be well on your way to building riches.

Focus on widening the gap between what you earn and what you spend. Obviously the more money you have while spending less the better your chances reaching your financial independence.

When you get unexpected money or a salary increase, do the same of your savings and investments increase the allocation to savings and investments. A wind fall does not mean you have to spend it, whenever you get that 13th check, bonus or performance options, and the more money you have saved for investment the better.

Pick one or two wealth building ideas at a time and focus on them. You are never going to walk 100 miles until you take the first step. To be a millionaire you aim to save that first dollar, then that first $100, then your first $1,000, $10,000 and so on. Make baby steps set goals from getting out of debt to specific amounts year on year.

Turn savings into investment capital because savings is only for safe keeping and inflation but for your wealth and money to grow you have to invest that money. Make your money work for you.

Understand that compound interest is one of your best allies in reaching wealth, as your money earns interest and your interest starts earning interest, the compounding effect.

There are many ways you can invest your money such as stock markets, real estate, businesses, and so on. Choose one and become an expert at it by studying hard and well. It's best when you have control despite your access to financial advisors.

Your home may contribute significantly in your net worth in the long run but don't look at your home as an investment. It's your biggest expense on a monthly basis. To unlock the value of your home means you lose your shelter so most people will not look at their homes as investments per say although it is an investment.

Budgeting is key to building wealth so you have to be careful how you spend money and never misuse any amount of money carelessly for entertainment purposes like lotteries and gambling. The possibilities or probabilities of wining large amounts of money are luring and can be very addictive. But never gamble thinking wining will solve many of your problems.

Invest little or big amounts, it doesn't matter as long as you have a long term investing strategy. When you start its easier to continue and grow, do not let the fact that you may not have a big enough capital stop you.

You are your best investment so investing in your education will provide you with many dividends, it pays and it's always the best investment.

Have an exit strategy with financial independence in mind. Plan to be independent by having a plan for how you are going to exit the workforce if you are employed and maintain your lifestyle comfortably. Don't be a paycheck hostage.

Don't follow spending trends, don't buy the latest anything because it's the latest or just to have it so people see you have it. Forgo living a consumer driven lifestyle. Spend your money on value appreciating assets instead of gadgets.

Wealth slips away from the individual who invests in things for which they are not familiar and don't have the skills to maintain. Invest in what you know and have passion for its easier to follow and more comfortable. When you have passion for what you do you hardly feel you are working in fact it becomes a pleasure to work

You are set back in terms of money and time, remember that all we have in life is time as the most precious commodity, so falling prey to scams will work against your wealth building. Avoid get rich quick schemes, they lead nowhere, you will instead by funding someone's lifestyle.

Know how much you are worth and see how well you performed year on year and set annual targets in terms of percentage. You can set a yearly growth rate from 10 to 100% of your wealth. Track your wealth. Know where you are and where you are going. You can't manage what you don't measure.

Wealthy people know their net worth, poor people couldn't be bothered.

We have internal protective mechanisms and we can generally instinctively sense danger. Trust your gut. It won't lie to you. No matter how good something looks on paper, stick to what you know.

Modeling is important as finding someone who is doing better than you or has been in your situation and managed to reach the level of wealth you aspire to is ideal. Find a mentor who is financially intelligent and listen to the advice, not a mentor who tries to sell you something. There are many book and motivational speakers whose job and wealth building strategy is to sell you as many books and programs as possible, look out for those and avoid them.

Guard your reputation, your name could be worth gold. Your character and public reputation needs to be maintained and protected from unjust accusations. Put a stop to defamatory statements, the press is notorious when it comes to negative reporting, to these people bad news is reportable news; that is why you will hardly hear positive reporting everything on the news is negative. People will choose to do business with or without you based on your reputation.

Life is a greater school than any university. Theoretical knowledge allows you to make decisions in life when facing various situations, daily life will teach you what you can never learn at school so be observant and learn from your experience.

Borrowed money is one of the most common ways otherwise smart people go broke.

Don't be too conservative. Take advantage of opportunities. Fear will lead us to seek less riskier ventures or opportunities available to everyone while riskier more rewarding opportunities no one wants to take on remain untouched.

Don't swing for the fences either. In investing, emotions are your greatest asset…and liability.

To build your wealth you need to be more proactive, more aggressive and more of a self-starter than anyone you know personally.

Work up a budget and then work that budget.

Take responsibility for your financial situation. You may not have caused it, but you are responsible for it.

Don't drive away your wealth. The majority of millionaires own their cars rather than lease them. Most are more likely to buy used vehicles instead of new.

Look where you want to go. Professional athletes imagine themselves making the winning shot over and over again. See yourself winning the financial game.

Income does not equal wealth. There are a lot of income rich people that are broke.

Pay attention to little things. Over time they add up.

Keep going with things get tough. It makes all the difference in the world.

Don't associate with toxic or aimless people. Soar with the eagles, not the buzzards.

Wealth is much more than your net worth. It's about meaning and purpose. It's about living life on your terms.

Having a set of daily, weekly, monthly, and annual net worth goals will put you far ahead of most people.

Time is money. Spend a lot of yours planning your financial future.

Wealth accumulation is largely a function of your financial intelligence. You must learn before you can earn.

Live like a "secret" rich person and you'll become one. Most millionaires don't live in sprawling mansions. They live well below their means.

Love the home you are with. Your choice of home and how often you choose a new one, will determine your ability to accumulate wealth.

Make your money hard to reach.

Reverse your thinking. Instead of saving what's left after spending, save for your financial goals first and then spend what you have left over.

Start saving for retirement right now. Not after you've saved for a house. Not after you've saved for the kids' college education. Start putting something away today.

Credit card debt is the tie that binds losers together. There's no way to get ahead financially when you're paying 21% interest.

Make your lifestyle lag your income, not the other way around.

Put wealth building on auto pilot. Setup as many automated deduction/saving systems as possible to eliminate having to make a choice when it comes to saving. Make it automatic.

Time is money. Millionaires never waste time doing things which are not bringing in more money. Little minded people will waste time doing things which will lead them to utter poverty.

Protect your principle. Don't put yourself in a position where you have to re-earn your nest egg.

Amateurs listen to stories on television. Professionals do the math.

You're no more likely to build wealth because someone sold you a get rich trick than you are to build a house because someone sold you a shiny new hammer.

Beyond the above mentioned you will also take note of self-improvement, continuous education and open mindedness, financial education or literacy is imperative these days. For those with religious faith it's been proven that religion can be a great source of mental stability and happiness. You can use your faith to insure that god allows you to stick to specific behaviors while working to reach your target. God wants you to live in prosperity, you can apply biblical, torah or koranic principles to your wealth building plan. There is a way to handling wealth building based on your religious principles, there is no religion on earth that wants you to suffer in poverty. It's a fact that the Christian bible has a lot to say about money, management of money, acquisition of money and wealth in general. Wealth or money is mentioned more than any other topic in the Christian Bible. Let's take a look at wealth building and money on a biblical perspective: reading the bible you can come across the fact that Wealth has been a blessing or a curse for a few characters in the bible. But it's not the money that's the problem, rather the attitude toward it. The wealthy is expected to be giving, humble and have gratitude toward God for all his blessings.

Even under biblical principles, a good budget will allow you to spend less or uncontrollably, decrease your debt, and increase your savings and investments opening doors for a lot of possibilities. Religiously when building wealth we are preparing for the next generation and to do this we need to plan and think and have a vision. With clear vision, we begin to think of our legacy for the next generation. The Bible says, "A good man leaves an inheritance to his children's children" (Proverbs 13:22). Biblically we are supposed to teach our children that God owns everything and we manage it for his glory that way wealth becomes generational. We begin to prepare our children to pass on their own positive legacy to future generations. Once you have secured your family's wants and needs financially you are to broaden your vision to include other families. We seek out ways to meet the needs of others, and we become cheerful, outrageous givers. When God blesses us this much, He expects us to use a portion of that wealth to serve others in his name. Yes, the money is a blessing, but it also comes with much responsibility. That responsibility includes giving, but it also involves debunking a few popular money myths for our own benefit and the benefit of our legacy. The Bible discourages debt every time it's mentioned. Proverbs 22:7 says, "The rich rules over the poor, and the borrower is slave to the lender." Without debt, think of what we could do with our money for the kingdom of God!

As we increase our wealth the bible cautions to avoid two critical spirits that are everywhere in our culture today. The one being jealousy and the other envy. Some people today believe wealth is evil and should be avoided at all costs. They unfortunately have the spirit of poverty which is rooted in jealousy and envy. Jealousy wants what someone else has. Envy thinks we can't get what someone else has, so we don't want them to have it either. Both are unbiblical, but both are tremendous temptations if we give in to the spirit of poverty.

Others struggle with the spirit of pride, which says that wealth comes from hard work alone. To defeat both of these spirits, we must nurture a spirit of gratitude instead. That means we display grace (rather than performance), focus on Jesus, and remember that wealth ultimately comes from him, and it remains his as the bible says.

When we're living with a spirit of gratitude toward God, we're practicing biblical principles in building wealth. That means living our lives every day acknowledging that every resource, every dollar, every second of time, belongs to God. It's all His, and we're His managers. We give freely because we don't own it. Giving isn't a salvation issue, but it does transform us. It allows us to praise and worship Christ, and it's a form of spiritual warfare. When we give cheerfully, God knows he can trust us with his money, so he can entrust us with more. This isn't a prosperity gospel, but it really is what often happens! The Torah, Koran and many other religious books will have similar views about money and management of money. This is an interesting way to look at money, management and its ownership.

When talking of wealth building and its principles, we already know that savings or savings accounts are only when you want to provisionally park your money until you make an investment. Investing once you have saved ideally in passive income instruments would be ideal especially if you can run a business or already have other activities. We make the following suggestions for earning passive, recurring or residual income; passive, recurring or residual income streams will always require an upfront monetary investment.

You can generate passive, recurring and residual income from the following:

The stock market, Dividend Stocks; you can earn good money through Dividend stocks this will require that you buy stock in large quantities to have significant return from the company. Peer to peer lending is not a wide spread practice but P2P lending is the practice of loaning money to borrowers who typically don't qualify for traditional loans, it's a higher risk but investors are earning 4-6% returns on average. Rental Properties will have you earn monthly but as previously said you will be required to purchase the properties therefore make a significant upfront investment. High Yield Savings Accounts and Money Market Funds available through must financial institutions. CDs (certificates of deposits) from banks in certain increments so that you can earn a higher return on your money. CDs are offered by banks and since they are a low risk investment they also yield a low return. Insurance companies have annuities on offer: Annuities are an insurance product that you pay for but can then provide you passive income for life in the form of monthly payments. The terms with annuities vary and are not always a great deal so it's best to talk to a trusted financial advisor if you're interested in purchasing an annuity. Invest In A REIT (Real Estate Investment Trust) These are investment vehicles that hold property within them and you as the owner get to benefit from the gains, refinances, sale, income (or loss) on the property.

Invest in a Business as an option to generate passive income as a silent partner.

There are many more products out there that can help you generate passive income. You need time and the ability to focus to really grow a passive income stream so chose one and master it before you had more. Don't spread yourself thin. As is the case for most investments it's going to take a substantial amount of time or money in the beginning but earning passive income is an excellent wealth builder, make a plan, and dedicate yourself until that income stream comes to fruition. To building long lasting wealth you have to study and develop your own principles of building wealth.

Get Rich Quick Build Wealth Now

Chapter VIII

Success & Inspirations

Success and inspirations can never be separated for they complement each other in everything we are and do. Success has to be inspired, we model our lives after people and very often aspire to be like many people. Many artists will always speak of the fact that they were inspired by another artist leading to where they are. The musician Michel J. Jackson a highly successful musical artist very often spoke of the fact that he was inspired by James Brown another artist from a previous era. Every generation is inspired by the previous generation.

I have personally been inspired by the following quote:

"Success is to be measure not so much by the position that one has reached in life as by the obstacles which he has overcome while trying to succeed." By: Booker T. Washington

This simply means that there are several degrees of success and everyone can feel successful at his level of achievement. Measuring success is made easy when you stack up and look at obstacles that one had to overcome to succeed. Many people have all it takes to succeed and success is very often made easy for certain people who as an example will have a job waiting for them after school while others will struggle and go to endless interviews. Well connected parents can offer privileges to their children that are not available for the average kid. In trying to encourage children at school very often teachers say: do the best you can shoot for the moon even if you miss you will still be amongst the stars. If you are poor and succeed in getting out of poverty into the middle class, you can be proud of yourself. If you are in the middle class and you break into millionaire status, there also you can best measure your level of success in life.

"If you can't fly then run, if you can't run then walk, if you can't walk then crawl, but whatever you do you have to keep moving forward." Rev. Martin Luther King, Jr.

This quote from Martin Luther King is very inspiring and very often when things get difficult in life, many people turn to a motivational quote for inspiration or to God for those who are religious.

Why rely on inspiration for success or for our aspirations and goals in life? Well let's look at the origins and definition of inspiration. Inspiration has a long history, originally thought of as coming from divine or supernatural forces. In ancient Greece, the Muses were goddesses who inspired the creation of literature and the arts by speaking directly with the human creators themselves. Perhaps due to the mystical connotations associated with the term, scientists haven't touched the concept until recently. In recent years, fascinating studies on inspiration have emerged, spearheaded by Todd M. Thrash and Andrew J. Elliot. These studies allow us to take something as seemingly elusive as inspiration and understand its operation and impact on other important psychological outcomes. As it turns out, inspiration matters a lot in our lives.

The Oxford English dictionary defines inspiration literally as "the action, or an act, of breathing in or inhaling". But in this book we are concerned with the figurative meaning: "A breathing in or infusion of some idea, purpose, etc. in to the mind: the suggestion, awakening, or creation of some feeling or impulse, especially of an exalted kind".

Keeping true to the spirit of this definition, Thrash and Elliot define inspiration as involving three main related qualities. First, inspiration is evoked spontaneously and without intention by something whether it's an idea that comes from within, an inspiring person such as a role model, or a divine revelation. Another key quality of inspiration is that it is transcendent of our more animalistic and self-serving concerns and limitations. Such transcendence often involves a moment of clarity and awareness of new possibilities. As the researchers note, "the heights of human motivation spring from the beauty and goodness that precede us and awaken us to better possibilities." This moment of clarity is often vivid, and can take the form of a grand vision, or a "seeing" of something one has not seen before (but was probably always there). Finally, inspiration involves approach motivation, in which the individual strives to transmit, express, or actualize a new idea or vision.

As a first pass to capture inspiration in the laboratory and see how it relates to other psychological constructs, Thrash and Elliot developed the "Inspiration Scale", which measures the frequency of experiencing inspiration. The scale measures inspiration as a trait, assuming that people differ from one another in the frequency with which they experience inspiration in their daily lives. In their initial set of studies, they found that trait inspiration (as measured by their Inspiration Scale) predicted people's ongoing daily experiences of inspiration and those who scored high on the Inspiration Scale also tended to score high on a range of other traits characteristic of inspiration: evocation, transcendence, and approach motivation.

In terms of evocation, trait inspiration was related to Openness to Experience and absorption (i.e., flow), but not Conscientiousness. This supports the view that inspiration is something that happens to you and is not willed.

In terms of transcendence, trait inspiration was related to the drive to master work but was negatively related to competitiveness, which reflects a non-transcendent desire to outperform competitors. Inspiration was also positively related to intrinsic motivation and negatively related to extrinsic motivation. Therefore, what makes an object inspiring is its perceived subjective intrinsic value and not how much it's objectively worth or how attainable it is.

In terms of approach orientation, trait inspiration was related to Extraversion and Openness to Experience, traits which are tightly linked to each other and have both been tied in prior research to the dopaminergic neurotransmitter system. Dopamine has mostly activating effects on behavior and cognition and contributes to approach behavior, positive affect, and sensitivity to rewards, broad thinking, and mental flexibility. Inspiration was also related to important psychological resources, including self-efficacy, self-esteem, and optimism. Importantly, many of the associations found with trait inspiration were also found when looking as inspiration as a state. While people may differ from one another in the frequency of their daily inspiration, anyone who experiences inspiration at any time can reap similar benefits.

The researchers also looked at outcomes. Trait inspiration was related to various majors, but showed its highest levels among students majoring in the humanities, such as art, religion, and philosophy all fields concerned with transcendent values such as beauty, goodness, and truth. There were also linkages to creativity. Those scoring high on the Inspiration Scale reporting viewing themselves as more creative and showed increases in self-ratings of creativity over time. Additionally, patent-holding inventors reported being inspired more frequently and intensely than non-patent holders, and the higher the frequency of inspiration, the higher the number of patents held. This link to creativity is consistent with transcendent aspect of inspiration, since creativity involves seeing possibility beyond existing constraints.

In terms of timing, Openness to Experience often came before inspiration, suggesting that those who are more open to inspiration are more likely to experience inspiration. Mastery of work, absorption, creativity, perceived competence, self-esteem, and optimism were all consequences of inspiration, suggesting that inspiration facilitates flow, creativity, and important psychological resources. Interestingly, work mastery also came before inspiration, suggesting that inspiration is not purely passive, but does favor the prepared mine. Inspiration was least related to variables that involved agency or the enhancement of resources, again demonstrating the transcendent nature of inspiration. Look to be inspired look for a role model to insure that you will have the additional strength or resource needed when down or farcing hardships.

Success is everyone's dream and there is no shortage of inspirations for anyone in any circumstance. Many successful people often have a guiding quote that inspire them throughout their life and as they reach the apex of their aspirations, develop quotes to inspire others. In terms of wealth building and for the purpose of inspiring you towards your objectives. We have assembled powerful inspirational quotes for you. Let these inspire you in any of your endeavors;

- If you have trouble imagining a 20% loss in the stock market, you shouldn't be in stocks. ***John Bogle***

- If you've got a dollar and you spend 29 cents on a loaf of bread, you've got 71 cents left; but if you've got seventeen grand and you spend 29 cents on a loaf of bread, you've still got seventeen grand. There's a math lesson for you. ***Steve Martin***

- If we command our wealth, we shall be rich and free. If our wealth commands us, we are poor indeed. ***Edmund Burke***

- The Stock Market is designed to transfer money from the Active to the Patient. *Warren Buffett*

- In a society in which nearly everybody is dominated by somebody else's mind or by a disembodied mind, it becomes increasingly difficult to learn the truth about the activities of governments and corporations, about the quality or value of products, or about the health of one's own place and economy. In such a society, also, our private economies will depend less and less upon the private ownership of real, usable property, and more and more upon property that is institutional and abstract, beyond individual control, such as money, insurance policies, certificates of deposit, stocks, and shares. And as our private economies become more abstract, the mutual, free helps and pleasures of family and community life will be supplanted by a kind of displaced or placeless citizenship and by commerce with impersonal and self-interested suppliers... Thus, although we are not slaves in name, and cannot be carried to market and sold as somebody else's legal chattels, we are free only within narrow limits. For all our talk about liberation and personal autonomy, there are few choices that we are free to make. What would be the point, for example, if a majority of our people decided to be self-employed?

The great enemy of freedom is the alignment of political power with wealth. This alignment destroys the commonwealth - that is, the natural wealth of localities and the local economies of household, neighborhood, and community - and so destroys democracy, of which the commonwealth is the foundation and practical means. **Wendell Berry, The Art of the Commonplace: The Agrarian Essays**

- A successful man is one who can lay a firm foundation with the bricks others have thrown at him. **David Brinkley**

- Don't let the fear of losing be greater than the excitement of winning. **Robert Kiyosaki**

- Develop success from failures. Discouragement and failure are two of the surest stepping stones to success. **Dale Carnegie**

- Believe you can and you're halfway there. **Theodore Roosevelt**

- Fortune sides with him who dares. **Virgil**

- You are essentially who you create yourself to be and all that occurs in your life is the result of your own making. **Stephen Richards, Think Your way to Success: Let Your Dreams Run Free**

- Do the one thing you think you cannot do. Fail at it. Try again. Do better the second time. The only people who never tumble are those who never mount the high wire. This is your moment. Own it. ***Oprah Winfrey***

- Being rich is not about how much money you have or how many homes you own; it's the freedom to buy any book you want without looking at the price and wondering if you can afford it. ***John Waters, Role Models***

- A journey of a thousand miles must begin with a single step. ***Lao Tzu***

- Rich people have small TVs and big libraries, and poor people have small libraries and big TVs. ***Zig Ziglar***

- Wealth consists not in having great possessions, but in having few wants. ***Epictetus***

- Do not go where the path may lead, go instead where there is no path and leave a trail. ***Ralph Waldo Emerson***

- If plan A fails, remember there are 25 more letters. ***Chris Guillebeau***

- Success is walking from failure to failure with no loss of enthusiasm. ***Winston Churchill***

- The Seven Social Sins are:

    Wealth without work.

    Pleasure without conscience.

    Knowledge without character.

    Commerce without morality.

    Science without humanity.

    Worship without sacrifice.

    Politics without principle.

    From a sermon given by Frederick Lewis Donaldson in Westminster Abbey, London, on March 20, 1925. ***Frederick Lewis Donaldson***

- I've been making a list of the things they don't teach you at school. They don't teach you how to love somebody. They don't teach you how to be famous. They don't teach you how to be rich or how to be poor. They don't teach you how to walk away from someone you don't love any longer. They don't teach you how to know what's going on in someone else's mind. They don't teach you what to say to someone who's dying. They don't teach you anything worth knowing. ***Neil Gaiman, The Kindly Ones (The Sandman #9)***

- Screw it, let's do it! *Richard Branson*

- Don't tell me what you value, show me your budget, and I'll tell you what you value." *Joe Biden*

- Before you speak, listen. Before you write, think. Before you spend, earn. Before you invest, investigate. Before you criticize, wait. Before you pray, forgive. Before you quit, try. Before you retire, save. Before you die, give. *William A. Ward*

- It's not how much money you make, but how much money you keep, how hard it works for you, and how many generations you keep it for. *Robert Kiyosaki*

- If you don't value your time, neither will others. Stop giving away your time and talents. Value what you know & start charging for it. *Kim Garst*

- It's good to have money and the things that money can buy, but it's good, too, to check up once in a while and make sure that you haven't lost the things that money can't buy. *George Lorimer*

- I never attempt to make money on the stock market. I buy on the assumption that they could close the market the next day and not reopen it for ten years. ***Warren Buffett***

- An investment in knowledge pays the best interest. –Benjamin Franklin

- I love money. I love everything about it. I bought some pretty good stuff. Got me a $300 pair of socks. Got a fur sink. An electric dog polisher. A gasoline powered turtleneck sweater. And, of course, I bought some dumb stuff, too. ***Steve Martin***

- Too many people spend money they earned to buy things they don't want to impress people that they don't like. ***Will Rogers***

- Opportunity is missed by most people because it is dressed in overalls and looks like work. ***Thomas Edison***

- Annual income twenty pounds, annual expenditure nineteen six, result happiness. Annual income twenty pounds, annual expenditure twenty pound ought and six, result misery. ***Charles Dickens***

- I will tell you the secret to getting rich on Wall Street. You try to be greedy when others are fearful. And you try to be fearful when others are greedy. ***Warren Buffett***

- Many people take no care of their money till they come nearly to the end of it, and others do just the same with their time. ***Johann Wolfgang von Goethe***

- Financial peace isn't the acquisition of stuff. It's learning to live on less than you make, so you can give money back and have money to invest. You can't win until you do this. ***Dave Ramsey***

- Empty pockets never held anyone back. Only empty heads and empty hearts can do that. ***Norman Vincent Peale***

- Buy when everyone else is selling and hold until everyone else is buying. That's not just a catchy slogan. It's the very essence of successful investing. ***J. Paul Getty***

- How many millionaires do you know who have become wealthy by investing in savings accounts? I rest my case. ***Robert G. Allen***

- Try to save something while your salary is small; it's impossible to save after you begin to earn more. ***Jack Benny***

- As long as you're going to be thinking anyway, think big. ***Donald Trump***

- What we really want to do is what we are really meant to do. When we do what we are meant to do, money comes to us, doors open for us, we feel useful, and the work we do feels like play to us. ***Julia Cameron***

- I made my money the old-fashioned way. I was very nice to a wealthy relative right before he died. ***Malcolm Forbes***

- Money is a terrible master but an excellent servant. ***P.T. Barnum***

- A real entrepreneur is somebody who has no safety net underneath them. ***Henry Kravis***

- Here's to the crazy ones. The misfits. The rebels. The troublemakers. The round pegs in the square holes. The ones who see things differently. They're not fond of rules. And they have no respect for the status quo. You can quote them, disagree with them, glorify or vilify them. About the only thing you can't do is ignore them. Because they change things. They push the human race forward. And while some may see them as the crazy ones, we see genius. Because the people who are crazy enough to think they can change the world, are the ones who do. *Steve Jobs*

- Wealth is the ability to fully experience life. *Henry David Thoreau*

- I'm a great believer in luck, and I find the harder I work the more I have of it. *Thomas Jefferson*

- You must gain control over your money or the lack of it will forever control you. *Dave Ramsey*

- Never spend your money before you have it. *Thomas Jefferson*

- Twenty years from now you will be more disappointed by the things that you didn't do than by the ones you did do. *Mark Twain*

- The question isn't who is going to let me; it's who is going to stop me. *Ayn Rand*

- When buying shares, ask yourself, would you buy the whole company? *Rene Rivkin*

- It is impossible to escape the impression that people commonly use false standards of measurement — that they seek power, success and wealth for themselves and admire them in others, and that they underestimate what is of true value in life. ***Sigmund Freud, Civilization and Its Discontents***

- Wealth is like sea-water; the more we drink, the thirstier we become; and the same is true of fame. ***Arthur Schopenhauer***

- The biggest challenge after success is shutting up about it. *Criss Jami*

- The only place where success comes before work is in the dictionary. ***Vidal Sassoon***

- People often say that motivation doesn't last. Well, neither does bathing – that's why we recommend it daily. ***Zig Ziglar***

- You can't connect the dots looking forward; you can only connect them looking backwards. So you have to trust that the dots will somehow connect in your future. You have to trust in something – your gut, destiny, life, karma, whatever. This approach has never let me down, and it has made all the difference in my life. ***Steve Jobs***

People who are generally more inspired in their daily lives also tend to set inspired goals, which are then more likely to be successfully attained. We cannot neglect the power of inspiration in our daily lives. Inspiration allows us to transcend our ordinary experiences and limitations and is a strong driver of the attainment of our goals, productivity, creativity, and well-being. Inspiration transforms a person from experiencing a culture of apathy to experiencing a world of possibility. This all happens without any shift in ability or skill, and in fact propels the level of ability that the person thought they were capable of.

This book must have motivated you and inspired you to go for your dreams and be the best you can be. The one quote the author shares with you will inspire you to know that there is no limit to anything you put your mind into. You have learned how to Get Rich Quick Build wealth Now.

You are not pre-disposed for something that was not meant to be.

Mbok Antoine

Get Rich Quick Build Wealth Now

Appendix & Resources

The Black Wealth Initiative. by BlackEnterprise.com January 1, 2000

URL. http// www.metlife-gulf.com Wealth Builder Brochure; American Life Insurance Company, Wilmington, Delaware, U.S.A.,

Rich Dad, Poor Dad by Robert T. Kiyosaki

URL http//wwwyouarecreators.org The Ultimate Guide to wealth and Prosperity! (Law of Attraction)
URL http;//www.danespotts.com Powerful min Secrets you must know! The key to Permanent Change (Law of Attraction) Persons Mentality, by Katherine Hurst
http://www.nlpacademy.co.uk/calendar/ Neuro-linguistic Programming origins

URL. Http;//www.investopedia.com "3 Simple Steps to Building Wealth" By Investopedia November 27, 2017.

URL. http://www.GoodFinancialCents.com .

URL. http://www.cnbc.com "Self-made millionaire: Forget skipping Starbucks. Here are 5 real ways to get rich" Grant Cardone 5th January 2017.

URL http//www.listenmoneymatters.com "how to Get Rich Quick Realistically" Written by Matt Giovanisci

Source of statistics: http://www.globalissues.org/article/26/poverty-facts-and-stats

URL http//www.briantracy.com Change Your Thinking! 5 Mentality Shifts Wealthy People Live By to Achieve Financial Freedom by Brian Tracy

http://www.pursuit-of-happiness.org/science-of-happinesss

URL http://www.crisismagazine.com/author/james-jacobs. The Meaning of "Life, Liberty, and the Pursuit of Happiness" by JAMES JACOBS_JULY 4, 2017

URL http//www.buildingwealth.org Wealth Building A Beginner's Guide to Securing Your Financial Future is produced by the Community Development Department and the Communications & Outreach Department, Federal Reserve Bank of Dallas, 2200 N. Pearl St., Dallas, TX 75201-2216. Content Curator and Writer Julie Gunter

URL http://www.forbes.com/sites/robertberger/ Top 100 Money Quotes of All Time Rob Berger 30 April 2014,

URL https://www.goodreads.com/ Wealth Quotes

URL http://ParaPublishing.com Book Writing Template by Dan Poynter © Copyright 2005, Dan Poynter Para Publishing, Dan Poynter, PO Box 8206, Santa Barbara, CA 93118-8206, USA. Tel: (805) 968-7277, Fax: (805) 968-1379,

   URL https://www.psychologytoday.com/experts/scott-barry-kaufman
   Scott Barry Kaufman is Scientific Director of The Imagination Institute in the Positive Psychology Center at the University of Pennsylvania.

Get Rich Quick Build Wealth Now

Bibliography

The bibliography lists the reference materials or sources used in writing the book.

The Black Wealth Initiative. by BlackEnterprise.com January 1, 2000

URL. http// www.metlife-gulf.com Wealth Builder Brochure; American Life Insurance Company, Wilmington, Delaware, U.S.A.,

Rich Dad, Poor Dad by Robert T. Kiyosaki

URL http//wwwyouarecreators.org The Ultimate Guide to wealth and Prosperity! (Law of Attraction)

URL http;//www.danespotts.com Powerful min Secrets you must know! The key to Permanent Change (Law of Attraction)

Persons Mentality, by Katherine Hurst

http://www.nlpacademy.co.uk/calendar/ Neuro-linguistic Programming origins

URL. Http;//www.investopedia.com "3 Simple Steps to Building Wealth" By Investopedia November 27, 2017.

URL. http://www.GoodFinancialCents.com .

URL. http://www.cnbc.com "Self-made millionaire: Forget skipping Starbucks. Here are 5 real ways to get rich" Grant Cardone 5th January 2017.

URL http//www.listenmoneymatters.com "how to Get Rich Quick Realistically" Written by Matt Giovanisci

Source of statistics: http://www.globalissues.org/article/26/poverty-facts-and-stats URL http//www.briantracy.com Change Your Thinking! 5 Mentality Shifts Wealthy People Live By to Achieve Financial Freedom by Brian Tracy

http://www.pursuit-of-happiness.org/science-of-happinesss

URL http://www.crisismagazine.com/author/james-jacobs. The Meaning of "Life, Liberty, and the Pursuit of Happiness" by JAMES JACOBS JULY 4, 2017

URL http//www.buildingwealth.org Wealth Building A Beginner's Guide to Securing Your Financial Future is produced by the Community Development Department and the Communications & Outreach Department, Federal Reserve Bank of Dallas, 2200 N. Pearl St., Dallas, TX 75201-2216.

Content Curator and Writer Julie Gunter

URL http://www.forbes.com/sites/robertberger/ Top 100 Money Quotes of All Time Rob Berger 30 April 2014,

URL https://www.goodreads.com/ Wealth Quotes

URL http://ParaPublishing.com Book Writing Template by Dan Poynter © Copyright 2005, Dan Poynter Para Publishing, Dan Poynter, PO Box 8206, Santa Barbara, CA 93118-8206, USA. Tel: (805) 968-7277, Fax: (805) 968-1379,

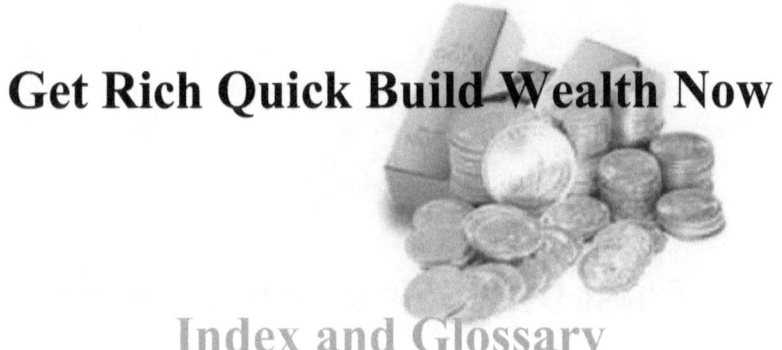

Get Rich Quick Build Wealth Now

Index and Glossary

Bloodline Entrapments, This term was invented by the author Mbok Antoine and defined as: biological and genetic weaknesses. Mental and physical limits we individually have as a result of biological and genetic weaknesses inherited from our parents or ancestors. **Page 81**

NLP, Neuro-Linguistic Programming, Dr Richard Bandler invented the term "Neuro-Linguistic Programming" in the 1970s. "a model of interpersonal communication chiefly concerned with the relationship between successful patterns of behavior and the subjective experiences (esp. patterns of thought) underlying them" and "a system of alternative therapy based on this which seeks to educate people in self-awareness and effective communication, and to change their patterns of mental and emotional behavior."

Modern day exploitative slavery class, people work very hard, but they never seem to earn enough and they are trapped in what seems to be a sort of servitude where they are hostage to living from paycheck to paycheck in the grip of poverty. **Page 27**

Get Rich Quick, Get rich quick is a suggestion that we should quickly be in a mental state of creating, growing and maintaining earnings so as to be rich, wealthy. **Page 25**

Get rich Quick, Build Wealth Now.

Trust that being rich is better.

"If this book does not get you rich, nothing else will."

Mbok Antoine

Very good motivational content.

ISBN (9781795293686)

© 2018 Minvestco Ltd

www.ingramcontent.com/pod-product-compliance
Lightning Source LLC
Chambersburg PA
CBHW021408210526
45463CB00001B/275